LOUIS BOUYER

WOMAN IN THE CHURCH

LOUIS BOUYER

WOMAN IN THE CHURCH

TRANSLATED BY
MARILYN TEICHERT

IGNATIUS PRESS
SAN FRANCISCO

Title of the French original:
Mystère et ministères de la femme dans l'église
© 1976 Aubier, Paris

With ecclesiastical approval
© Ignatius Press, San Francisco 1979
All rights reserved
ISBN 0-89870-002-7
Library of Congress catalogue number 79-84878
Printed in the United States of America

To Elizabeth Goudge

*With a friendship of
more than twenty years
and an admiration that
goes back even further.*

CONTENTS

PREFACE   9

CHAPTER

I   A Female Priesthood?   11
II God and Woman   29
III Woman in Creation and Salvation   40
IV Complementary Vocations of Men
    and Women   47
V   Traditional Feminine Ministries   71

CONCLUSION   89

APPENDIX   93

   Legislation and Influence   95
   The Consecrated Virgin
      in Today's World   99
   Religious Vocations Today   106

Epilogue *by Hans Urs von Balthasar*   113

Priestesses in the Church?
              by C. S. Lewis   123

PREFACE

The potentially disruptive controversy over the ordination of women to the priesthood, which is becoming widespread within the Church, should have at least one beneficial effect. It should lead us to a deeper understanding of the mystery of woman. The fifth chapter of Ephesians and the twelfth chapter of the Book of Revelation, among other Biblical texts, attest to the crucial importance of this mystery for a right interpretation of the Gospel. However, it has not yet received the attention it deserves. The exploration of this mystery offers, without doubt, the most positive way to confront the current flood of sexuality which is even more unbalanced than unbridled.

It is certainly no coincidence that the calling into question of the constant refusal of Jewish and Christian tradition to allow a feminine priesthood (or rather an asexual priesthood, open to women and men without distinction), is taking place precisely in an era which is so obviously unsettled with respect to sex roles. The strangely sophisticated motives alleged by the partisans of radical change, their ignorance and evident misunderstanding, bear clear witness to the depth of the general uncertainty regarding the true place and essential role of women in society: in a word, of what constitutes feminine dignity, a concept completely alien to what one hardly dares any more to call our civilization.

To examine and criticize these false lines of reasoning, the worst not always being the oldest, would seem the simplest and most natural way to clear away the prejudices which encumber the issue. From there one may proceed to reexamine the mystery of woman in all its authentic aspects.[1]

---

[1] The most complete treatment of this problem, leading to what we see as the solution, has been furnished, we think, by the symposium edited by H. Karl Lutge, *Sexuality, Theology, Priesthood*, to which Anglicans, Catholics, Orthodox and Protestants have contributed, published by "Concerned Fellow Episcopalians" (1973). A debate for or against, in the framework of a general revision of the theology of the priesthood, was organized, also by Anglicans, in San Francisco. The principal contributions appeared in another anthology, *To Be a Priest* (1976). Particularly notable is the contribution of Michael Marshall, now Anglican bishop of Woolwich, which was of great help to us.

CHAPTER I

A FEMALE PRIESTHOOD?

We generally hear that the refusal to ordain women to the priestly ministry (that of bishop, or of priest of the second order) stems simply from an outmoded conception of the inequality of the sexes—of the invincible inferiority of woman to man. And then it is claimed that if Christ himself, and the apostles after him, called or ordained only men, it was because the prejudices of their time would not have permitted them to do otherwise, whether because they did not believe they could successfully oppose these views or because they were incapable of extricating themselves from them. Finally it is said that even if Christ did not call women to the apostolate, this no longer has any more lasting significance for the Church than the fact that he called only Jews. Just as Christianity, when it emerged from the Jewish world, conferred the priesthood on non-Jews with no problem, so in our day, having emerged from a society characterized by exaggerated male predominance, it would no longer have a single good reason to refuse ordination to women.

To those of our contemporaries who know nothing of the history of mores and ideas, these reasons might appear irrefutable and even self-evident. But when we inquire more deeply into the facts and reflect on the motivations they reveal, we can see the extreme fragility, not to say total inconsistency, of such apparently sound reasoning.

Let us look first of all at the second of the above affirmations: that society at the time of Christ in particular, and of antiquity in general, would not have been able to accept the ordination of women to the priesthood. It is astonishing to hear people who believe themselves to be enlightened and free of prejudice come out unabashedly with such an enormity. In point of fact, from the earliest civilizations of the Fertile Crescent through the Greece and Rome of the early Christian era, the ancients had always been accustomed to female priests who were not in the least in an inferior position to male priests. This was true particularly, but not by any means exclusively, of the Mediterranean world. And if there was any particular tendency in this regard at the time of Christ and his apostles, it was much more in the direction of validating rather than rejecting the priesthood of women. In the mystery religions which began to spread at the same time as Christianity or very shortly thereafter, and which in the third century, just before its victory, showed themselves to be Christianity's last and most fearsome competitors, one observes in fact a recrudescence in the development of women priests. This happened in connection with the cults of goddess-mothers (divinities of fertility of the sun who were transformed into deities of the future life) which constituted one of the most notable religious characteristics of that era.

If, therefore, infant Christianity, despite all the ways in which its practices might have been opposed to those of Judaism because of its desire to be open to the pagan world, nevertheless retained the traditional Jewish and Biblical idea that the priesthood is an exclusively masculine domain, it was not at all due to a concession to prejudices current in the milieu within which it was propagated. On the contrary, it stood in decisive opposition to the mores which society in general considered to be self-evident.

It should be added that if Judaism itself, following the course of the ancient Hebrew religion, adopted and maintained a contrary posture towards the universal practices of popular religions when Biblical revelation intervened, its opposition was the more flagrant in order to form a people whose religion was completely different!

This fact is so obvious that anyone at all conversant with the history of comparative religion, especially in the ancient Semitic East, is obliged to find another explanation. Thus it is said that if, at its beginning, the Mosaic religion rejected the priesthood of women, this might be explained by noting the fact that women priests, tied as they effectively were to the naturalistic fertility cults and their orgiastic rites, would bring with them inadmissible practices like sacred prostitution. The unfortunate thing is that this explanation either explains nothing or proves too much. As a matter of fact, these practices, including sacred prostitution, were not at all limited to women priests. They were equally prevalent among male priests. If, therefore, one could thereby explain the fact that the Hebrews refused the feminine priesthood, which appeared to them tainted by these practices, it is difficult to see how they could have, in those conditions, admitted a masculine priesthood either, which at the time and in the milieu in which they lived bore just the same stains.

We must thus recognize honestly what the evidence itself suggests: when one studies, in historical and cultural context, the developments of religion, first Hebrew, then Jewish, and finally Christian, it becomes obvious that it was not at all through unreflective adherence to the practices and prejudices of their contemporaries that the Christians, following the Jews, heirs themselves to the Mosaic traditions, remained constant in refusing the priesthood to women.

A Female Priesthood?

On the contrary, this stance was constantly held in opposition to what practically the whole ancient world considered normal. We do not see in Jewish and Christian tradition, as some would have us believe, the effects of a simple assimilation of uncritically accepted customs. Rather it is definitely the result of a very deliberate and singularly persistent "No." Even if the theory was not yet elaborated, this was not due to the absence of principles. It was the result, on the contrary, of an extraordinarily constant fidelity, despite all the pressures of custom and cultural environment, to a stubbornly retained principle.

To this, naturally, will come the reply: but if there is an underlying principle, what would it be if not the idea of inequality—the invincible inferiority of woman to man? Here again the doubtful character of the reasoning strikes us, perhaps more forcibly than ever. The religion of the Bible, then Judaism and even more clearly Christianity in their turn, even if they did not constitute the only tradition of antiquity where the equality of man and woman was maintained (above all in the religious sphere, but also in the whole realm of creation), proclaimed, and defended, did constitute unquestionably the most firm and consistent tradition on this point. And if, after all, this equality appears today to be axiomatic, no serious historian would dream of contesting the fact that this is a result of Christian preaching, for which all of Judaism and the entire Bible to which it appeals paved the way.

To be sure, it is no less essential to Christianity, as to all of Biblical tradition, to affirm that woman, to be equal to man, must nonetheless remain different from him. In other words, this equality is not one of pure and simple identity, but rather of a positive and fruitful complementarity. Furthermore, as we shall see soon, it is precisely this safeguard of necessary complementarity, without which the pretended equality of woman would be nothing but an annihilation of her originality and proper identity, which motivates the limitation of the priestly ministry to men.

For the moment, however, let us confine ourselves to pointing out the absurdity of a position which explains the exclusively male priesthood of the Hebrews and Christians as a result of a conception of woman as inferior. Such an idea is quite contrary to the Bible and more specifically the Gospel, which alone assured woman's equality in a world in which nevertheless the priesthood had never been reserved to men as it has always been in the Church as well as in Israel.

This is accentuated by the fact that in Israel, where the role of the prophets was a major one and could even be said to have been of much more consequence than that of the priests, the

A Female Priesthood?

function of prophet does not appear to have been reserved to men. Even if relatively few women were recognized as possessors of the gift of prophecy, there was not a trace of opposition raised against them when they did appear to have it.

In a more general sense, when one seriously examines the traces that have been found in the Bible or in ancient Judaism of the apparent discrediting of women, one finds quite the contrary to be the case. What is the meaning, for example, of the "purification" to which women were submitted on the fortieth day after the birth of an infant male, or to which men themselves were subjected after sexual contact with a woman before being again allowed to take part in religious rites?[2] Was this really based, as some people claim, on some idea of the fundamental impurity of woman which would "soil" a male who came into contact with her? Such interpretations, from the standpoint of scientific religious phenomenology, are not only ridiculously naive, but are exactly contrary to the facts.

In order to clarify this point, let us first recall that in the same way, according to the most ancient Jewish tradition, simple contact with the scrolls of the Torah, or with an inspired book, "soiled the hands." In this same archaic sense,

---

[2] Leviticus 12:25, and all of chapter 15.

the traditional Christian liturgy speaks of "purifying" the sacred vessels, when it is in fact a matter of removing all traces of the consecrated elements.

This is the key to the laws dealing with sexuality, and specifically with woman's role in it. It is not that there is any impurity here. It is on the contrary that there is something sacred: sexuality is the creaturely manifestation of God's life-creating activity while the woman is the instrument of this participative creativity. Whence the suspicion, the presumption of possible sin whenever fallen man comes into contact with them, just as in his contact with the very signs of the Divine Presence. Is he not always tempted by lack of faith in the divine Word, by infidelity to the divine plan it represents and promotes?

In this case as in the other, if there is any hint of corruption, it is nothing but the *corruptio optimi*, which is clearly the *corruptio pessima*.

Likewise, what conclusions have not been drawn from the blessing which the rabbis taught men to pronounce, giving thanks that they have been "made men, and not women"? What is forgotten is, first of all, that these same people adjured women in like manner to bless God for having been made as they are.[3] What,

[3] See the text of these benedictions and their commentary in the treatises, *berakoth* of the *Mishnah* and of the *Tosefta*.

in fact, is the meaning of both these blessings? It is, as the same rabbis never ceased to explain, that the whole yoke of the Torah, and in particular the priestly functions, the *abodah*, the sacrificial service, were imposed solely upon men who were only too tempted to balk at the supplementary requirements it entailed. Therefore, it was necessary to inculcate into them the idea that these requirements, as onerous as they were, were to be accepted by them as an honor. Reciprocally, women, toward whom God manifested the liberality of his mercy even more than the severity of his justice, had but to offer to God a pure act of thanksgiving for the vocation which was theirs.

This, however, does not at all mean that women were excluded from religious practice. It was simply that they were not the ones upon whom the responsibility for the public practice of religion devolved, though at the same time they took part in it on an equal footing with men. Their responsibility was for the fundamental cell of the people of God—the home —which, for Israel, remains the first and last of sanctuaries. In this role it was up to the women to prepare the Paschal meal, the Biblical sacrifice par excellence, as well as every sacred meal, though they were not the ones to preside over it, their task being rather to light the candle on the Sabbath.

This suffices already to demonstrate that the

differentiation of roles already present in the Old Testament does not imply any inferiority of woman, but rather an indispensable complementarity between the sexes. That complementarity itself implies, as we shall soon see, that woman has a much more immediate and constant relationship of intimacy with the sacred than does man. This is why, although in the Bible and in the Jewish and later the Christian liturgy God is always spoken of as a male, Wisdom, which still signifies the closest conceivable association of mankind to divine thought and even divine life, is always represented by Israel as feminine. More remarkable still, if possible: the immanent presence of God, not only with man but in him, is always described by the rabbis with the feminine traits of the *Shekinah*.[4] But the most remarkable instance of such usage, we must add, is what we call the "Spirit" of God—that is to say, the communication to man of the divine vitality and energy whereby we are initiated into God's own life and activity. In Hebrew, as in other Semitic languages, this Spirit is designated by the feminine, not the masculine, substantive *Ruach Adonai*.

In view of these historical givens, which have served as the proper coordinates for the exclu-

---

[4] We have devoted a study to this notion in *Bible et vie chrétienne* (December, 1957) 7 ff.

A Female Priesthood?

sively male priesthood from the Old Testament era, throughout the history of the Church and up to our times, one can no longer assume that we are dealing with a fortuitous phenomenon, explicable by virtue of transitory contingencies, but corresponding to no intrinsic necessity in the nature of man and woman.

It is quite true that numerous theologians and Biblical scholars today tell us that, if the traditional distinction has undeniably endured throughout Biblical and Christian history, this nevertheless does not in itself constitute a theological justification for it. In matters of this kind, they tell us, we are dealing with a question of discipline, of expediency, not of principle. Thus, if the Church were to decide that it would be good, in our changed circumstances, to grant the priesthood to women, as it has been good not to do so in the past, there would be nothing to prevent it.

This kind of reasoning is singularly inconsistent. The perseverance of the Church, following all of Scripture, in maintaining a certain mode of action contrary to the common practice of mankind, if it were not substantiated by a fundamental principle, even if it had remained more or less implicit up till now, would be both incomprehensible and unjustifiable.

In fact, the reservation of the priesthood to men (*viri*) quite certainly rests on a theological principle made explicit—if not with exact definition, at least unambiguously—since the beginning of revelation. Those who are apparently unable to see this, if we are to judge by their actions, would in the same way have said before the Council of Nicea that the genuinely divine Sonship of Jesus could not be considered a theological principle, since it was necessary precisely for this council to define it by the consubstantiality of the Son with the Father. The same people, using the same type of reasoning, would have declared the divinity of the Spirit theologically indefensible before the Council of Constantinople, or the unity of the person of Christ before that of Ephesus, or the complete reality of his two natures, human and divine, before that of Chalcedon, etc.

Behind their affirmation, there is a view of theology which one would have to call slothful because it is completely static, the result of a narrow, literalist view of revelation. We have here what makes all the narrow conservatives involuntary allies—but unfortunately most efficacious ones—of heretical innovators, in virtue of an inertia, an absence of reflection which considers itself an expression of piety. In this particular case it does not appear exaggerated to say that, if one cannot simply produce a clear text or argument to refute an opponent, neither could this have been done when the divinity of

A Female Priesthood? 23

Christ was being disputed. The length and the difficulties of the Arian controversy demonstrate this well enough. It is precisely for this reason that the first Ecumenical Council had to define it.

But in the present case as well, the massive *consensus fidelium* of more than twenty centuries is, in fact, supported by a superabundance of Biblical teaching and of Christian spiritual experience which could not escape any but the most myopic view of the texts and the facts. This leaves us in no doubt about the final decision the Church would have to make, the definition of her faith on which she would have to support herself if the authorities were to find themselves pinned to the wall by the adversaries of tradition.

Let us add that in the present case, behind the Christian and Biblical understanding, there is a natural, spontaneous view of sane humanity which a simple, well-founded and scientifically developed anthropology would have no trouble formulating and justifying. In fact, the recent call for the ordination of women in order to assure the equality of women and men supposes that this equality cannot be obtained except by as radical an effacement as possible of the differences between them. Yet, according to the most informed psychologists and sociologists, this is a symptom of the particularly unfavorable conditions in which this problem of the equality of the sexes is posed by modern man. Following this path of equalization, what they want to promote risks being ruined from the outset because the problem is posed, without their realizing it, in unrealistic, self-defeating terms. The apparent victory which they would win in such circumstances, far from assuring them their hearts' desire, would be its veiled defeat.

We find ourselves in this case in the presence of a form of feminism which, well-intentioned as it might be, can only be destructive of true liberation of women. For equality which is confused with pure and simple identity with another (while he is, of course, your equal, but for all that, not identical with you) could not possibly be anything but a delusion. It could only result, for those who insist upon it, in the final loss of their own identity.

This is what we have seen very clearly recently in the United States, in the context of a completely different but analogous issue: racial equality. The most intelligent and realistic black leaders became aware of it in time, and the formulation of the problem was modified completely within a few years. Whites of good will, followed at first by the most naive blacks, believed they were offering them perfect equality in proposing pure and simple integration into their own society—a society completely formed by whites, according to their own tastes.

But the most alert blacks, upon reflection, were not long in noticing that such integration, for them, far from signifying the liberation they hoped for, could not have led to anything but the complete destruction of what they are and what they want legitimately to remain. Even supposing that it could ever have succeeded, it would not have made the blacks, as blacks, equal with whites, but rather shamed blacks, hiding behind a mask of pseudo-whiteness which would not fool anyone. Hence this reaction, apparently paradoxical, but fundamentally very realistic and profoundly sane, of the black leaders who, in America today, do not hesitate to say that an integration of the blacks into white society in the manner in which it was first conceived would in fact be worse for them than the apartheid of South Africa. In point of fact, even if the latter implies their inferiority, or in any case points up their perpetual minority, it begins at least by recognizing their identity. The proposed form of integration, however, in pretending to ignore their identity as blacks purely and simply, if it had been attempted, could only have tended toward abolishing it. Systematically applied and followed, it would result in the most radical form of genocide.

As the great Dutch psychologist Buijtendijk[5]

[5]*La Femme*, by Buijtendijk, has been translated into French.

has demonstrated perfectly, it is the same, *mutatis mutandis,* for every simplistic kind of feminism which sees no other means to equality of women and men than to masculinize women. This amounts to the suppression of women as such. Feminism of this kind, if it were to triumph, would only be a Pyrrhic victory for women. It would in fact signify the definitive triumph of a most obtuse and absurd kind of masculinity.

This is what is tended toward, *volens nolens,* in the current supposition that the equality of woman and man could be affirmed and consolidated by the ordination of women to the priesthood. Far from producing its desired effect, the endeavor would be nothing but a particularly unreasonable manifestation of this kind of essentially self-defeating feminism. For one cannot entertain the idea of ordination of women except by a misunderstanding of the mystery of woman which is inherent in her own identity. Such a lack of understanding would result in undermining her dignity and finally reach the point of denying her the right to exist.

It is no coincidence, let us be assured, that the same era which pretends to equalize woman with man in granting her the priesthood is an era in which we see woman relegated, to an unprecedented degree, to the role of a simple object of pleasure for the idle male. In the one case as in the other, in fact, the tendency is to deny woman all that is properly hers, not to recognize in her any value but one which is borrowed, either in total dependence on the male, or in complete confusion with him.

In opposition to the one as to the other, an analysis of the mystery of woman which underlies Scripture and all Christian tradition should avoid crushing her femininity through the conferring of a ministry for which she is not fitted, and should lead us to discover (or to rediscover) the ministries which are proper to her, and for which she is fitted—ministries which it is surely important for the Church and the world of today finally to grant to woman—or simply to restore to her.

What we have just said should make it already perfectly clear that it is important to reconsider and rediscover more deeply than ever the mystery of woman, not in order to diminish woman's role in the Church and in the world—and certainly not to diminish her dignity as woman—but on the contrary to recognize the indispensable grandeur of this role, the unique beauty of her femininity. One of the keys to the crisis which both the Church and the world are facing today (and paradoxically the Church perhaps more than the world) is simply the current misunderstanding of this mystery which, despite superficial appearances to the contrary, is more confused than ever. In stark contrast, the mystery of woman, throughout the Bible and Church tradition, is presented as the final mystery of creation, especially redeemed creation, saved and made divine by the Incarnation of God in flesh which he took from a woman.[6]

---

[6] Despite innumerable vulgarizations, most of them hasty and superficial, of Freudian sexuality, it is astonishing that there are so few serious theological works to be found which treat this question. However, we may cite the excellent study of Derrick Sherwin Bailey, *The Man-Woman Relation in Christian Thought* (1959).

CHAPTER II

GOD AND WOMAN

The mystery of woman, precisely because it is the mystery of creation redeemed, completed and espoused by God himself, presupposes the mystery of God and cannot be understood without reference to him. However, the mystery of God is not at all, for all that, simply the reverse side of the mystery of humanity. To put it better, it encompasses the mystery of man (*homo*, man and woman) as well as of *vir* (the male), but it surpasses it and in such a way that the mystery of woman in particular finds its source there, a source wherein one might say it is reflected, but, as in every reflection, reversed. We must begin by sorting out, as much as possible, this paradox to which we are driven by the properly Biblical knowledge of God, in order to see the mystery of woman in proper perspective. Thus the ministries of man and of woman both will be seen in their proper places.

It is sometimes said, and it is true in a sense, but only in a sense, that God, the God who has spoken to us through Biblical tradition (as opposed to the ancient Near Eastern divinities who were so heavily sexualized), appeared to transcend the division of the sexes. It is suggested, too, that he unites in himself the most exalted characteristics of both woman and man. This is not without some justification, but nevertheless it cannot be admitted as a truly satisfying expression of his revelation.

Many of the great gods in pre-Columbian America and other archaic civilizations are said to have been seen as both "fathers and mothers" of humanity—indeed, of everything. Certainly the same Hebrew prophets who paved the way for the New Testament revelation of the divine Fatherhood did not hesitate on occasion to compare God, in the solicitude and the intimacy of his love, to a mother who would never abandon her children, so much is children's being of one flesh with their mother's. But never did the Bible go so far as to say that God was "our father and our mother," and it is impossible for anyone who is familiar with what one could call the gist of his whole revelation to believe that this is a chance omission or simply a momentary stage before the revelation reached its fullness or was explained by the Church. The God of the Bible is "Our Father," and even more is he "The Father," "the Father of our Lord Jesus Christ and our Father,"[7] so much so that his Son, in becoming man, made us also "sons," as St. Paul

---

[7] See the salutation of most of the letters of St. Paul.

says, or "children" of God, as St. John puts it.[8] But Jesus has no other mother than a woman, the Virgin Mary. And if we ourselves, by virtue of our natural adoption, have a mother who is our mother more truly than Eve, the "Mother of the living,"[9] this can only be the entire Church, represented, or rather, as we shall see later, realized par excellence in the same Virgin Mary, the only one who is both Jesus' mother and our mother.

It is perfectly true, on the other hand, that if Mary realizes this motherhood which is not only proper to a creature, but in which all her possibilities are realized, beyond her, yet in the trajectory of her creaturehood, God is not simply the perfect expression of an essentially human fatherhood, extended as we might imagine it. He is Father in a completely different way than any man could be, so much so that, far from fatherhood appearing to be an essentially human state in the sense that motherhood is, it is, in man, on the natural plane, at most only an incomplete image, indeed, one subtly contradictory to that which it is in God. And when it is a matter of attributing supernatural fatherhood to a man, despite the warning of Jesus,[10] one must certainly not forget that such fatherhood is not a property of those by whom

[8] I John 3:1
[9] Genesis 3:20.
[10] Matthew 23:9 and parallels.

it is exercised, but a simple representation in them of the divine fatherhood. In this sense, they are the bearers or conductors of it, but not really the owners of it.

As St. Athanasius observes,[11] being a father is never, on the part of a man, more than one quality among others, and it is only momentarily that even he who becomes a father exercises the role in fact. On the other hand, the divine Person who is the source of divinity itself, and as such the sole first cause in the most radical sense, not only exercises his fatherhood eternally, but defines himself by this fatherhood which is always in act. In the case of the heavenly Father, fatherhood is much more than a function: it is a subsistant relationship by virtue of which everything subsists which ever shall subsist.

This already is tantamount to saying that that which is most truly divine in God, if we may put it this way, is expressed in man (*homo*) by the polarity between man (*vir*) and woman, yet nevertheless surpasses and transcends man just as much as woman, to the point that man (*vir*) as such seems incapable of becoming complete in himself. This is, in fact, true in two senses. On the one hand, the fatherhood of man cannot be realized without woman, not to say in woman. But on the other hand, he is not dis-

[11] Athanasius, *Contra Arianos I*, 18–19; 1st epistle *ad Serapionem*, 17 and *Contra Arianos II*, 29–31.

tinguished from her or opposed to her in the relation by which they complete one another, except by this representation of one greater than he; he is himself nothing more than a touchstone and he will never do better than to evoke, without ever truly assimilating, the fatherhood which is only properly realized in God. For fatherhood, in its whole and true sense, can be nothing other than divine, since it is the quality of being a source—the source of all beings as of one's own being—and therefore of pure being, always in act. Even masculine spousehood itself, we shall see, as it derives from the association of creature to creator which is brought about by the divine Word alone, is only fully and primarily realized in his incarnate person.

More simply and profoundly, as St. Gregory of Nyssa[12] saw so clearly, the divine fatherhood, the only true fatherhood worthy of the name, is essentially virginal. In other words, far from presupposing a complementarity—the joining of man and woman—God's fatherhood is anterior to this distinction. But, it must be added, if there is nevertheless some analogue to this fullness, expressed in the distinction of the sexes and surpassing them, we do not find it in man (*vir*). Just as with fatherhood, so virginity in man can only be predicated in an approxi-

---

[12] Gregory of Nyssa, *De Virginitate*, II; PG 46, col. 321 C.

mate, imperfect sense. On the natural, created plane, it is only woman who can claim true virginity. The unmarried woman, in fact, contains, in herself, at least potentially, all future humanity, both masculine and feminine, for it will never come to being if not by an interior development in the feminine being which the male does nothing but set into motion, playing, again, only a representative role, at most as a transmitter of the creative initiative which remains purely divine. Even if this initiative happens to pass through him, one can never say it belongs to him, whereas in woman, on the contrary, the creativity received from on high is carried, and at the same time is exercised within her and remains with her. It follows that in woman physical integrity has a completely different meaning and a different reality than in man. What one might improperly call virginity in man is only a matter of not exercising a potential fatherhood, which, even when he is called to exercise it, still does not truly belong to him, for it is in him always a matter of a single instant in which he still does not become the source, but rather a momentary channel of fatherly creativity. In woman, on the other hand, this integrity is the unmitigated fullness wherein exist all the possibilities of human developments *in potentia*, since they will simply be developments of her being.

God and Woman

We already see, therefore, that God, inasmuch as he reveals himself supremely as *the* unique Father, appears in certain regards as a masculine being, and not feminine: no more bisexual than asexual, although the masculinity of man only expresses itself in man as a trait not only derivative but borrowed, and never wholly realizable in him. Even on the physical, natural plane, to say nothing of the supernatural, man will never be more than a father by proxy, in a sense, nor will the whole—even what is in fact essential—of fatherhood ever be in him. There is only one father who is entirely a father, and that is God.

Here we must make more precise what has been implied thus far. That is, that if man is capable of being more truly a spouse, in the sense that he effectively realizes and completes himself in union with his wife, he only does so in dependence upon, or, as it were, within the archetypal union of the eternal Word with divine Wisdom, accomplished through the marriage of Christ and the Church. This wisdom, in fact, is none other than the plan of God for his creature, and for the union of the creature with him—for which it was created. This is why it is in creation itself that this wisdom is truly realized, from beginning to end: first in the Virgin Mary, lastly in the entire Church. But woman, and each woman in particular, as woman, not only represents but realizes in her virginity something of that same integrity which is proper to the Virgin at the origin (and as the creaturely origin) of salvation history, and which will be that of the Church when it has achieved its completion in time. In the same way, as spouse, each woman realizes in herself something of the feminine spousehood, the fullness of which is the Church. And as mother, her motherhood is that motherhood whose perfection is Mary.

There is, therefore, in the masculinity of man, something incomplete and incapable of completion except in the Son of God become man. Even Christ's masculinity is not complete, except by virtue of the fatherhood from which he proceeds; but Christ as man nevertheless exceeds and transcends humanity, even divinized humanity. We must therefore say definitively that man, the male, is not truly man except in the heavenly Man,[13] the Son of God. Further, the only true and integral fatherhood is, strictly speaking, neither masculine nor feminine, since it belongs exclusively to the only Father who is solely and integrally father, though he realizes in an equally transcendent fashion that virginity which finds its earthly, human image only in woman.

As paradoxical as this all may seem, it already

---

[13] Corinthians 15:45 f.

shows us in what sense sexuality is transcended in God, or rather anticipated, not in asexuality —even less in bisexuality—but in a fatherhood and sonship which transcend the opposition of the sexes and to which masculinity is like a shadow and femininity like a reflection.

This last point is borne out, in relation to the Father, in feminine virginity, the only creaturely integrity in which limitless potentiality responds to the total actuality of the uncreated; and it is borne out again, in relation to the Holy Spirit, in motherhood.

We have already mentioned the fact that in Hebrew, Aramaic and Syrian, as well as in other Semitic languages, the word "spirit" is feminine. The writings of the Syrian fathers, particularly Aphrates,[14] rightly emphasize that this fact is not insignificant. This linguistic affinity reveals precisely what we have characterized as a reflection, but a reversed reflection. Let us reiterate that it is the role of woman to encompass in her motherhood all that is human, masculine or feminine, just as we can say it is all pre-contained in her virginity. We can find no other analogy in the created order for the relation of the Spirit to that which it inspires. However, the analogy here, in contrast to that which we drew between human and divine fatherhood, is not so much a question of

[14] Aphrates, *Demonstratio* 18:10; *Patrologia Syriaca*, v. 1, 839.

incompletion or imperfection as it is of inversion. This is doubly true. In fact, in the case of the Spirit, it is the inspiration which seems to be within the inspired, while the child is within the mother. Moreover, the proper development of the child takes place only in its tending toward separation from the mother—the leaving of the womb. Even though he remains dependent upon her who gave him birth, the child must, to be truly himself, leave the mother's womb and let the umbilical cord be definitely cut. In the case of the Spirit, on the contrary, the perfection or consecration of the one inspired presumes not some kind of independence from the one who inspires, but on the contrary, the total and unreserved consummation of their union: what William of St. Thierry calls the *unitas Spiritus*—unity even more than union.[15] And this, borne out as true by human experience of the Spirit, can, of course, be verified only in a transcendent sense in the subsistence of the Spirit in God himself, in the womb of the Trinity. The fatherhood of the Father is not perfected, nor the sonship of the Son consecrated there, except by this proceeding of the Spirit from the Father, coming to rest forever in the Son.

Now, perhaps, we begin to glimpse the profundity of the paradox which encompasses all

---

[15] *Epistula Aurea*, II, cha. II, part 11.

the analogies which permit us to represent in some way, not an entirely misleading one, however inadequate it remains, the life and being of God in relation to our created life and being. Thus we begin to discern how God, under one aspect, is not properly speaking masculine, but reveals himself first, certainly, in the axis of a masculinity that transcends itself. And at the same time, in that which constitutes the perfection of his Trinitarian life (i.e., the processions of the Spirit), he contains in himself no less what we have called a reflection of woman in her proper perfection, which is also the perfection of humanity, indeed of all creation. But this reflection, like all reflections, is inverted. Or rather, if you prefer, there is in God, as it were, the antitype of what is reflected in reverse in the motherhood in which alone woman is wholly revealed, in particular a virginal motherhood. It is in this sense, certainly very subtle but also disconcertingly profound, that God is neither man nor woman, though he encompasses from the beginning all that humanity will ever bring to realization. He goes beyond masculinity in the only fatherhood worthy of the name, and is at the same time, in his eternal virginity, the antitype of all motherhood.

CHAPTER III

WOMAN IN CREATION AND SALVATION

It is equally remarkable to note that the greatest Hebrew prophets reject the idea of attributing sexuality to God—an idea which appears to be taken for granted among all the neighboring religions of their time—as the worst kind of blasphemy, the grossest kind of idolatry. Yet they do make use of it, though transfiguring it, where it is not a question of the life, the existence, the being of God, as he is in himself, but rather of the relation he desires to establish with his creature and which he desires the creature to establish in return with him.

The great message of the prophet Hosea is that Israel, the people of God, viewed then evidently as a feminine entity, is called finally to invoke God not as "my Baal," that is to say "my Lord" in the manner the Canaanite or Babylonian gods were addressed, but rather "my Spouse."[16] No one will underline with more emphasis than Hosea's from the very outset the completely gratuitous character of the unparalleled and almost inconceivable grace of

[16] Hosea 1 to 3.

this calling. But it is nonetheless clear for all that—in fact it is the more manifest for it—that the prophet insists on his affirmation being taken absolutely seriously.

From this there follows, already in the Old Testament, an unmistakeable transfiguration of human marriage and human sexuality, whose necessary ethical implications are fully developed only in the Gospel.[17] But this transfiguration, far from dissipating the realism of the analogy, consecrates it. This is manifestly clear in the great Biblical epithalamiums: Psalm 45 and the Song of Songs. There will always be a certain naiveté in the perplexity of the critics who have never ceased since the rabbinical era to ask whether those passages deal with an actual espousal between a man and a woman or rather with the union of the Lord with his people. Most certainly they deal with both: with the one within the other. Such a high idea of love and sexual union proceeds from the fundamental idea that it is worthy to represent the union of a God, even as transcendent as the Biblical God, with his creation—though the union of the sexes, in all its indissolubly carnal and spiritual reality, appears conversely not only as a possible image but as the only sufficient image of a union which is itself so transcendent.

We need not be surprised that Jeremiah, the

[17] Matthew 19:3 ff., and parallels.

prophet par excellence of the intimacy of God with his people, should have taken up this theme in his turn.[18] Even more than Hosea, he emphasizes in it the agonizing, even crucifying aspects. Reading him, we find ourselves on a developing line of thought which culminates in the declaration of St. Paul: "Christ loved the Church, and sacrificed himself for her."[19]

Ezekiel, in turn, took up the theme again even more boldly.[20] He emphasizes not only the infidelity, but the original unworthiness of the spouse, and, conversely, the limitless munificence of such a betrothal. He does this by revealing behind the spousal theme the even more radical theme of the fatherhood, uniquely God's, which is extended to man in the unimaginable and truly unbelievable grace of his supernatural adoption.

However, already in the Old Testament we find this theme of the marriage of God to his people twice re-echoed and expanded, which demonstrates to what point God is affected by it even though the envisaged relation has no place in God considered in his transcendence, but only on the level of his creative work.

In the first place, the Wisdom Books apply the theme to Wisdom herself, in her relation to the wise man in general, but especially to the

[18] Jeremiah 2 and 3.
[19] Ephesians 5:25.
[20] Ezekiel 16.

Wise Man par excellence, indeed, the only Wise Man worthy of the name: God. Wisdom is a feminine figure already in Proverbs 8; the final object of love for the wise man according to the Wisdom of Solomon;[21] Wisdom in Sirach[22] is undeniably the divine spouse. But what is this Wisdom, more and more concretely personified as the realism of the relationship with God becomes more intense? One might say that, seen in relation to the transcendent God, indeed in himself, it is his plan for all of creation. But if it appears in such a relation to him, it is because this plan is a plan of love, and very definitely of spousal love, where mutual knowledge demands the conformity of creation with the plan of its Creator, in a conformity to him which could only be the effect as well as the necessary condition of a true union of him who is everything with her who is nothing.

The rabbis, in their turn, go one step further with their theology of the *Shekinah*—the presence of God among his people in this world, which was already oriented by Ezekiel toward a presence in them.[23] Yet this was already implicit, at least, in the great text of Sirach where Wisdom appears as being one with this Presence under the luminous cloud which filled the Tabernacle and later the Temple.

[21] Wisdom of Solomon 7 ff.
[22] Sirach 24.
[23] Ezekiel 11:16.

In other words, the Wisdom Books assure us that this spousal relationship is not simply an accomodation to humanity, to its own modes of relational existence, which God makes in approaching us, but that it embraces in man, in humanity inseparable from the whole cosmos and revealing in its own history all the virtualities of this cosmos, the total and ultimate relation of God to all his works. Before God, finally, the whole creature is called to realize fully what we may call its femininity in a spousal vocation, which in turn brings out in God himself the character of supernatural Spouse.

The rabbis, however, we repeat, did nothing but bring into broad daylight all the implications of what was already latent in the wisdom writings. In fact, if it is truly real, this final relationship of the Creator to the creature supposes a reciprocal immanence. As we have been, we are and shall always be eternally in God, the unique object of an eternal love, all together and all things with us: God the Father, the invisible, as inaccessible as he is in his transcendent virginity, makes himself in us—in this other Self which is the spouse—immanence itself. He will remain in her at the end of time, as before time she remained in him. Therefore—and the rabbis, again, discerned this as the final implication of the divine Word—the Word itself, the *Memra*, is also feminine insofar as it projects creation outside of God, and at the same time calls it back to him in an ineffable intercession, but freely, as the final object of his love.[24] And this is to be seen already in Ecclesiastes again, where Wisdom and the presence of God are seen as one only when they are finally identified with this Word emanating from his eternal silence.

Insofar as it expresses the Name of God, however, the Word is one with the mysterious "Angel of the Lord" of the ancient Biblical accounts, which is really not separate from him, though it is distinct from him.[25] It is this which the Greek Bible was to express by applying to the Word the masculine noun, "Logos." Beginning with Philo there arises the first affirmation that this Logos is the first-born of God, in a sense his only Beloved.[26] Yet insofar as it expresses *ad extra* the love which is the life of God itself, the eternally fruitful life in the eternal virginity of his heavenly fatherhood, the Word is indeed feminine. For it expresses the will of God to call forth being from nothingness in order to espouse it in his eternal Son. Thus the cosmic city, where the elect shall be gathered together in the fullness of time,[27] where all

[24] See the *Targums* on the Song of Songs, 1:3 and 6:3.
[25] See, for example, Judges 13:3 ff.
[26] Philo, *De posteritate Caini*, 63; *Vita Mosis*, v. 2, 134; *De Confusione Linguarum*, 63.
[27] Revelation 21.

things shall be united around risen humanity, regenerated at the divine source, shall be revealed on the last day as the *Unica Sponsa*, consecrating in herself, in the reunion of Wisdom with the Word, the adoption with him and in him of all things by the Only Father from which all fatherhood, in heaven and on earth, receives its name.[28]

[28] Ephesians 3:15.

CHAPTER IV

COMPLEMENTARY VOCATIONS OF MEN AND WOMEN

All this might appear at first glance to be pure speculation—vain babbling about the invisible, the unutterable. In fact, as it is with all Biblical revelations when contemplated, these glimpses of heaven only lead us through faith into the heavenly realm when we come to discern with a higher vision of reality—not less but more realistic for being thus transfigured—the true sense of earthly things. These glimpses project a light on masculinity and femininity, on the relationship between them, on the division and nonetheless the equality of the sexes, a light which alone permits us to go beyond the simple surface of one of the most mysterious realities of our daily experience—indeed, of our very experience of our own being in relation to the world and to one another.

Marriage (the stable union of man and woman) undeniably acquired its dignity and full meaning only after having been consecrated in Biblical revelation by its incorporation into the relationship God willed between man, in all his reality, and himself. In the same way it was necessary for us to have been borne to these heights in order to understand the whole meaning of the communal life of man and woman. From that source flow the ministries, the services which, although transcending them both, they must nevertheless perform for one another as together they become the servants of the only true God and of the plan of love which concerns them in their native relationship to each other.

We have here a supreme example of this saving, regenerative faculty of the divine Word. In restoring to human things all their meaning and purity in order to elevate them to God, it clarifies and confirms them, and at the same time opens up in them unexpected perspectives, surpassing all our hopes—everything which man, reflecting on his own experience, could surmise as most true and most profound about himself.

It would seem that, after all we have said here, we might easily summarize what we can see more clearly about human nature by virtue of this supernatural illumination. But obviously the implications and consequences of this insight into man's nature are inexhaustible, and we cannot attempt here to envisage them in all their fullness.

Nevertheless, we will content ourselves with saying that man, the male, insofar as he is such, is defined by the following paradox: he essentially represents that which goes beyond him, which he is incapable of being in and of himself, in which he cannot even take part except by his participation through grace in the sonship of the only eternal Son, who himself represents the Father from whom he proceeds and from whom all things proceed: God in the inexhaustible vitality of his absolute transcendence. But, once again, on the natural plane, man is able to be a father only in a very partial and ephemeral way, while on the supernatural plane he can represent divine fatherhood only through his dependence on the unique image of the Father which is the only begotten Son.

Woman, on the contrary, simply represents the creature in its highest vocation, by which it is conjoined with God himself in his creation and even in his fatherhood. She *is*, potentially, in her virginity, all that she represents, and she becomes it effectively in her motherhood when she gives it reality within herself. For motherhood is the consummate association of the whole created being—the most intimate and efficacious conceivable—with that which one might call the very soul of divinity: the vivifying power, the fruitfulness of the Spirit. In motherhood she can attain to the most perfect assimilation possible of the created into the uncreated: the divine sonship by participation, in the consummation of the created Bride by her union with the divine Bridegroom. It is this which will be realized in fullness at the end of time, in the Church, as a universal echo of that which has been accomplished perfectly in the course of time in the virginal motherhood of Mary—a truly divine motherhood. Yet it is this which every woman, insofar as she is a woman and if she lives up to her vocation to womanhood, approximates on the natural level and accomplishes on the supernatural level in accepting, like Mary, God's entire plan for her.

What has just been said bears explanation, or, more simply, clarification, yet we might say that in it lies the crux of our whole problem. Created being, and particularly created personality, presents not only a vestige, but a veritable image of the uncreated in the freedom which it achieves. This is most clearly evidenced in the human personality, in which the material is assumed by the spiritual, which reciprocally not only conditions but defines it. And this freedom in the created personality is not simply passivity, i.e., sheer possible consent, given or refused, to a being received from without. In living out his proper existence on the simple natural level amidst all the possibilities open to him, and even more on the supernatural level, where he participates in the life of God as it is in God himself, man exercises real, positive activity, proper in the truest sense of the word to him who initiates it, even though it will always be secondary in relation to divine creative activity.

Complementary Vocations

But is this ever manifested or realized better than when it is not only a matter of effectively being or becoming all it is in one's power to be, but beyond that, of associating oneself with the very activity, proper to the divine Being alone, of bringing into existence beings other than oneself? Man is fully himself only when he thus participates as far as he is able in the activity of creating. Certainly, he never becomes an autonomous creator by means of this participation, but he is then an authentic pro-creator, not only in the sense of representing or transmitting creative activity, but by being associated—or rather by being allowed or invited to associate himself—with it.

Here again, however, we repeat that among all the modes of activity of which man (*homo*) is capable, the fullness and perfection of this activity of procreation can only be attained in woman, insofar as she is defined by her capacity for motherhood which, in her virginal state, is in itself unlimited. The supreme manifestation of this is the virginal motherhood of Mary, the divine motherhood, where humanity gave birth to God's own Son through the person of the woman par excellence, the integrity of whose virginity was thereby consecrated.

Man, the male, on the contrary, though he may appear more directly associated with this divine creative activity and fruitfulness because he is capable of being a father, never exercises, even on the natural level, any more than a momentary, radically incomplete paternity. He is its bearer or transmitter much more than its cause. The realization or completion of paternity, in fact, always operates outside himself, in the womb of the woman, whereas the source, by which fatherhood defines itself, remains beyond him, in God alone, man being in this aspect simply a channel.

This is even more evident in the man's supernatural participation in divine fatherhood, where he never plays more than a representative role. All the "spiritual sons" which a "man of God" may more or less legitimately claim, have in reality, as Jesus reminded us, no other true father but him from whom all fatherhood takes its name.

On the other hand, the Church is true mother to them all, and, within the Church, the Virgin most eminently. But the soul of every woman in the state of grace takes part in this motherhood, each one to an extent known to God alone. The souls of males are, of course, involved here too, but not at all by virtue of their masculinity, rather by virtue of the feminine element they bear within themselves. For, as the myth of androgyny suggests, and as modern science has verified, masculinity and femininity are inseparable in each human individual, although the masculinity or femininity proper to each individual results not from a simple predominance, which would only be quantitative, but rather from a polarization

Complementary Vocations

which makes everything which relates to one of the two characters gravitate around the other. But only in woman does the character of creaturely activity appear in its full purity; only in her is this activity entirely genuine, proper and truly personal, although—or better, precisely because—it is a derivative activity, manifesting itself as such.

The whole physiological being of woman, as opposed to that of the male, verifies this. And remembering that the soul of man is simply the substantial form of his body, we must expect that his physical being will reveal and define his metaphysical being itself.

In all the activities proper to him, and therefore in his sexual activity, man the male (and, of course, woman as well) reveals himself in and by his self-actualization. But it is both his greatness and his weakness that he realizes himself only thus, outside himself: only by detaching himself from that which he procreates. And where he reveals himself, in many respects he does so only by consenting to forget himself. One might, to that extent, hold that the male does not possess his own consciousness, for his consciousness is completely outward-directed, *ad extra*. What clearly proves this is that while it struggles to turn back upon itself, to grasp itself, inevitably it does so only by falling into a subjectivism where it loses itself in losing all reality.

In woman, on the contrary, these oppositions

hardly exist; insofar as she is woman, they have no point of entry. The being in relation to which she reveals herself best, surrendering herself to the greatest extent, is not in fact a being who becomes separate and alien to her. It is a being whom she carries within herself, whom she nourishes from herself, in which she grows and completes herself by reproducing herself. We have already indicated that it is, of course, necessary in order for woman's motherhood to achieve its goal that she also consent to a separation, to becoming autonomous of the being she has produced. For her there is a rupture, an inescapable separation which a man cannot experience. The consent to this separate existence of her children is much more difficult for her to accept by virtue of her very nature than it is for the man, on whom it hardly makes an impact: he is not even completely aware of it, since for him the process is simply a matter of course.

By virtue of this fact, the mother's consent to the birth is not only much more meritorious, but much more effectively gift-like. The result will be twofold: to the exact extent to which he has become truly himself, the child will freely, but all the more really, begin, by virtue of this gift, to experience himself as always dependent, not only on the materiality or the bodily existence of his mother, but on that which is the most spiritual in her: her own freedom, intimately associated to the act of creation in that gift where she surpasses herself in another. Likewise for the mother, despite this separation, or indeed from the very fact of her freely giving the consent she had to give: the gift given, because it is a gift, becomes more truly hers, but in a purer and higher sense which the male is incapable of achieving by himself. In the human creature, however, it is this that approximates most closely its own relation to the Creator: we are never so close to God as when we are completely ourselves, being his children in his only Son, and as St. John says, not only being called sons, but being sons in all truth.

The result of this is something which belongs so exclusively to feminine sensibility and to the very intelligence of woman that men, males, will never completely comprehend nor, ordinarily, even begin to grasp it exactly. It is what they mean when they say that women are incapable of objectivity, of a disinterested knowledge of things apart from themselves. It is quite true in a sense, but not in the way in which it is usually interpreted. For there is precisely this difference between the male and female intelligence: that the former is perpetually tossed between an objectivity which always risks becoming rigid and lifeless in detaching itself from the spirit, and a subjectivity fascinated by the abyss of subjectivism: a subject absorbing itself in a self which can never grasp itself except indirectly. Woman, on the contrary (even if she does not always realize it, and in fact rarely realizes it in a completely satisfying way), instinctively escapes this dichotomy because of her natural constitution. She is natively adapted to empathy, to that sympathy with the object which is not conceivable except in a subject such as only the feminine subject is, for whom the object does not appear from the outset as exterior. For, once again, everything in the feminine being is dominated by the constitution which makes her capable of carrying and forming another being originating in her own—a thing totally unknown and very difficult for a man to imagine or conceive of, since he is radically unsuited to all experience of this order.

The masculine being can therefore be said to be essentially intermediary, and by this fact indefinitely polymorphous, but also fundamentally unstable. The feminine being, on the contrary, represents, in the realm of the created, the goal, the achievement, the totality. From this proceeds a unity which can relapse into amorphousness in the woman who lives unreflectively, "lets herself go," as they say. But in the woman who is in possession of herself, while giving herself without reserve, this becomes the organic unity of all reconciliations, or simply conciliations, and more profoundly, the unity of a perfection found not in some voluntary limitation, but in a fullness which liberates both herself and others.

Complementary Vocations 57

This is the true meaning of the widely misunderstood words of St. Paul that "man is the head of woman as Christ is the head of the Church."[29] This does not signify submission, even less degradation of woman before man. We can only understand the true meaning of it by enunciating the reciprocal truth: as Christ completes his corporeality only in humanity as a whole, by the universal expansion of the Church, man truly assumes a body, a body totally human, only by and in woman. Although the male has necessarily to go beyond himself to realize himself, his body is only an instrument of contact which transmits what comes from a source higher than he. It is in the female body alone that the seeds are meant to germinate, nourished by the substance of the woman herself, to grow of her and in her and to mature there. This is translated to the spiritual level (which is by no means to say the disincarnate level) by the fact that the being of woman is the only being, on the level of the created world, where presence to self and presence to the world, presence of the world in its entirety, can become one. Man, the male, never finds himself except by a process of discovery blemished by narcissism, and, except by and in woman, he never meets the world in an encounter which is real communion rather than a

---

[29] Ephesians 5:23.

simple confrontation. The world is never real for the male except by symbiosis with woman. It is, moreover, by that alone that man attains the consciousness of himself which is not a solipsistic absorption, but the discovery of this identity as participation in the divine image.

On the other hand, woman needs the stimulation, the productive restlessness which only a relationship with man can give her, for lack of which the riches of the human unconscious, which resides most properly in her, will never reach the level of her voluntary consciousness, any more than man would be able to nourish his own consciousness, so quickly exhausted although never sated, if not in a fruitful relationship with woman.

In this relationship, such as it can and should be, woman reveals herself for man as more than the companion he dreams of, more than the complement he needs: she is revealed as the only place where he becomes himself by being completely human, and so the only place where, experiencing his total reality, he gains access to totally real being. It follows, then, that it may be said without hesitation that man needs woman in order to encounter God. The male, in the final analysis, is borne up by the total Presence, the divine Presence, as if drawn from beyond himself. But God is fully united with him only when he achieves harmony with the entire cosmos, and woman is not only the indispensable instrument, but the predestined locus for this encounter.

This is the problem which lies unobserved behind a tedious discussion which has divided moral theologians of the past generation: is the procreation of children the only primary end of marriage, or should the "mutual fulfillment of the spouses," as they put it, also be recognized as another, more than secondary end? The question is, in fact, meaningless. To persist as they have in attempting to resolve the question one way or the other can lead to nothing but the complete dissolution of the Christian (and human) view of marriage which we are witnessing today.

The truth is that, according to the point of view one adopts, woman can be considered as achieving her fulfillment either as spouse or as mother. But the two roles presuppose and inform one another, although their respective fulfillments are situated on different levels. This is why either supposition—whether of procreation (even one which is spiritual as well as material) pursued independently of the union of the spouses, or of union pursued independently of procreation—is equally unreal, and in fact devoid of meaning. It is in common procreation as such that the spouses are fulfilled as spouses by one another. Conversely, procreation which did not proceed from a genuine spousal relationship already achieved in each other would not be truly procreation, but would rather be reduced to a totally dehumanized act of physical generation.

In the same way, to take a new paradox, the eschatological vision of the marriage of the Lamb makes the role of Spouse appear to us as ultimate, in the consummation of the union of the Woman—and, in her, all humanity, all creation—with the heavenly Bridegroom. However—and here the reality of created freedom, its participation in creation, and even its own creation, is affirmed—she becomes the spouse only in her virginity, finally restored[30] despite a whole history of sin which is progressively assumed, recapitulated and converted into the history of salvation. This occurs at the completion of the cosmic event of giving birth, where St. Paul shows us the whole of creation echoing the ineffable groanings of the Spirit and itself groaning from a painful and apparently unachievable act of parturition.[31] The birth will come, in fact, only with the Parousia of the Spouse, who will come like a thief in the night when he is no longer expected. But it is precisely because of this long period of expectant maternity, so laboriously accomplished, that redeemed humanity will appear on the last day as the Spouse, chosen from the beginning and restored forever to an unalterable virginity.

[30] II Corinthians 11:2.
[31] Romans 8:22.

Complementary Vocations 61

Thus, we are finally in a position to discover the integral meaning of feminine virginity, and at the same time to understand how, in Mary, this virginity was consummated without being tainted by the fact of her motherhood of grace, her divine motherhood, whereas in the Church at the end of time this motherhood by grace will be consummated in the restored virginity of the morning of creation "when the sons of the dawn sang with a single voice."[32]

In order to arrive at this meaning of virginity, we must begin by understanding how and why it applies to womanly virginity alone—the only virginity on the level of creation which truly merits this name. Teilhard de Chardin once let slip the unfortunate remark that physical virginity, in and of itself, was of no particular value. Etienne Gilson's pertinent criticism[33] has pointed out the naiveté of this remark in its very masculine sufficiency. It is particularly astonishing, we might add, coming from a man who has so insisted on the spirituality of matter! In fact, if there is any place where it can be seen that the spiritual—in man in general and in woman in particular—is not separate from the physical, the corporeal, it is certainly here. Both as man and as woman, the human being is capable of becoming all things insofar as he has intelligence, an intelligence by its na-

[32] Job 38:7.
[33] E. Gilson, *Les Tribulations de Sophie* (1957) 96.

ture incarnate. But here we must repeat that the objectifying intelligence of man (*vir*) corresponds to a type of activity which directs him immediately outward and has this effect only by making him go out of himself. For woman, on the contrary, the essentially empathetic knowledge which we have tried to describe corresponds to a mode of activity proper to her which is carried on most fruitfully not outside but within herself. And this encompasses in each woman what is perhaps the most profound center of her mystery: the whole of created human reality with all its inexhaustible richness, but first of all in its organic unity, is initially present in the microcosm of her body as a shadowy perception which awakens her spirit.

The encounter with man is doubtless necessary to actualize and make explicit in detail this limitless potentiality. But, as this encounter takes on an inevitable aspect of investment, intrusion and breakage, its effect would no less inevitably entail not only a fragmentation, but an impoverishing reduction where the latent infinity which woman bears within herself gives way to a fragmentary finitude, and where her femininity is exhausted without ever being able to reveal itself completely. Only the betrothal of the divine Word with human nature in the womb of Mary, producing the very Son of God made flesh, realized this infinitude, and it therefore follows that the divine motherhood of the Virgin, far from staining her virginity, consecrated it. Even more marvelously, the consummated marriage of all humanity with divinity in the eschatological Church, by bringing about for all humanity and in all creation this realization of infinity in finite totality, will regenerate the virginity of creation in the consummation of the motherhood of grace.

All the preceding is clearly only a rough, very imperfect and sketchily drawn outline of the perspectives which the Biblical revelation of the Christian mystery par excellence (the mystery of Christ and the Church, of man and woman before God and in God) opens up for the essential mystery of femininity. Surely much more could be said about this theme, and doubtless much could be improved upon in this first sketch we have traced. But, imperfect as it is, it seems that it can still lead us to some important reflections which are the necessary prelude to any examination of the particular ministries—whether of men or of women—and of the cooperation to be hoped for among them.

If the preceding has any meaning, it is that only by and in woman does humanity become complete. Certainly, in order for that completion to come about, it is necessary that there be revealed to humanity one among us of whom man, the male, is, as it were, the already-prepared sign, in the predestined Head of humanity which is Christ—the perfect man, the heavenly man, the eternal man—because he is the Son of the divine Father and his only perfect image. But, reciprocally, if human nature finds its essential and its supernatural perfection only in the humanity of Christ, the male prototype of all masculinity, the human person finds initial unsurpassable perfection in a woman: the Virgin Mother Mary. And all human persons, in their common salvation, will not attain their own proper perfection until they converge at the end of time in the ultimate personality of the eschatological Spouse, "the Church of the first-born whose names are written in heaven."[34] She shall not have given them birth in grace, in the course of the history of salvation, except to appear herself at the end of time—or rather beyond all history—in the glorious virginity of the Betrothed of the Lamb, descended from heaven, from the right hand of God...

But the end of time is, in a sense, also our beginning. For it will be the recapitulation, accomplished in Christ, of all our history, of which St. Paul writes and which St. Irenaeus illustrates so well.[35] This presence *a retro* of the

[34] Hebrews 12:23.
[35] Cf. Ephesians 1:10 and Irenaeus, *Adversus Haereses*, III, 16, sec. 6 in particular.

Word becoming incarnate is a presence which moves man, the male, toward a truth which only takes form ahead of him little by little under his eyes, because at the root of his being it is already obscurely present and urging him forward. And this presence is revealed only in woman. This truth is present in her from the very outset in a form of consciousness which is uniquely hers, but which is neither the unconscious (which a man cannot try to grasp within himself without being submerged in it) nor the excessive consciousness which he pursues outside himself like a mirage and which escapes his grasp or condemns those who attain it to die of abstraction. The feminine consciousness of humanity is a glimpse—in the bright darkness in which Christian faith is at home—of that prenatal, virginal reality of divine Wisdom as it actually exists only in the womb of God, but as having become all of creation, completed, saved and transfigured at humanity's final parturition of itself and of the whole world with itself, which is our history redeemed, recapitulated and consummated by the divine Incarnation.

This is why woman seems to be naturally religious while man must become so—and, a still more difficult thing, remain so by a constant effort of pursuit or indeed to regain lost ground. A rabbi recently explained to me, with humor not devoid of meaning, that the Jewish law prescribes religious obligations for men, while it does not impose anything definite on women, and he observed that, far from supposing some superiority on the part of man, it implies quite the contrary: that he would not serve God if God did not take the trouble to recall him constantly to the task, while woman does not need anyone to tell her to do these things.

This, to be sure, does not imply any automatic merit for woman; for her as for man the value comes in the personalization of her gifts. For her this orientation toward the religious is an initial gift, intuitively perceived or sensed, but which demands a free acceptance. For man it is a gift to acquire, the motive of the activity which pushes him to go out of himself. But self-complacency, a typically feminine temptation, like superficial activism, a temptation no less typical of men, has its price. All the false mystical experiences, all the doubtful ecstasies which are ultimately only egoistic enstasies, make women their favorite prey and find in them all the fertile soil they need to prosper and proliferate. On the other hand, one might ask oneself whether the true mystical experiences, which owe to man (recall St. John of the Cross) the unbending critical verification of their authenticity, would ever have retained his attention, or even have become part of his experience, without the intervention of woman.

Simply think how many men there are who owe the first awakening of their spiritual life, and indeed its decisive maturation, above all to

Complementary Vocations 67

a mother, a sister, a fiancée or a wife. And one might ask oneself if those whose individual history appears to contain nothing of this sort (and they are rare) would have experienced this awakening or growth without all that the anonymous heritage of innumerable women has contributed to human tradition, to the life of the intellect and the heart, without which this tradition would not be what it is.

It is not without meaning that Greek rationalism, and the final impasse it reached in the emptiest kind of skepticism, was the product of the intelligence of a society which had made itself almost exclusively masculine. Nor is it chance that the unrealized promises of Plato's *Symposium*, which were only revived by Plotinus for a single hour of ecstasy without future, were put by Plato himself in the mouth of Diotima, just as it is in the conversation at Ostia that they live again, finally immortalized for Augustine, that is to say, in the wake of a mother opening heaven for her son simply by being transported there herself.

In the same way, our technocratic world, where God appears to be dead, but where it is really man who is outliving himself, is typically a world where rational—i.e., masculine—intelligence, dominates almost exclusively and, as an inevitable result, has relegated feminine intuition to the level of sub-human, blind instincts. Those who, like Jung, believe that modern man will not rediscover his soul until he reintegrates the *anima* with the *animus* are not wrong on this point.

On the other hand, as a typical example, among many others, we must recall that in the fourteenth century, when the scholastic intelligence seemed to be similarly enervated, it was the impulse of contemplative nuns which led Eckhardt and his Dominican disciples—who would not have otherwise escaped being rationalists inebriated with abstraction—back to the humble rediscovery of the light of mysticism beneath the cloud of unknowing.

Here again, the existence of a faculty does not necessarily entail its good usage, and it is clear that the Montanuses have their Priscillas, just as John of the Cross his Teresa or Francis de Sales his Jeanne de Chantal. The fact remains that for men no sprituality, good or bad, seems to go beyond pious impulse or avoid being dried up in systems if a feminine presence or influence does not intervene. Even the religious geniuses who may seem to us the most masculine—Evagrius Ponticus or Newman, for example—by their own admission would have stopped short of the religious, or been diverted, either toward sensuality or rationalism, without their encounters with Melanie or Mary at the decisive moment.

Historians of Buddhism are openly astonished to find that the figure of Buddha, where it has ceased to appear as a pure expres-

Complementary Vocations 69

sion of totally negative spirituality and has become the expression of the loving compassion of the saint (which goes far beyond the condescension of the sage), has been transmuted into the feminine figure of Kwanin. If they had gone a little more outside their limited frame of reference they might have spared themselves this astonishment!

It is well known that Gottfried Arnold constructed a whole history of Christian spirituality on this theme. He unwittingly caricatured his discovery by confusing the revitalizing mystical resources of faith with a relapse into simple sentimentalism; but even in doing this, we see that it was by a very masculine sort of confusion that he discredited the thesis of his own work. The work itself nonetheless retains a very real value: the male never finds or rediscovers the trace of God without some feminine contribution, even if it be also true, on the other hand, that the sources where woman seems to need and await men—like the Samaritan woman who awaited Jesus at Jacob's well— always risk being lost—indeed, *she* risks being lost—in the sands of dream or sensuality if he does not appear in time, or does not dare to reveal himself to her.

For, to make a final point, it is incontestable that this instinctive piety of woman has its counterpart in man. If there is a natural religion, it belongs to her. But among fallen humanity all natural religions tend of themselves toward magical or idolatrous paganism, and many times both together. It is man's part to purify those sources he is incapable of bringing forth on his own. Again, without what we call supernatural faith, lacking the constructive criticism of natural religion which only revelation can offer, tempted by himself to confuse purity with puritanism, man will purify the wellsprings woman reveals to him only by evaporating them.

CHAPTER V

TRADITIONAL FEMININE MINISTRIES

As incomplete and imperfect as they are, the preceding reflections suffice to clarify very precisely the strong foundation of the traditional practice of the Church concerning the granting of the episcopal and priestly ministry to males only. This is so evident that it might appear superfluous to enumerate ponderously the inevitable practical consequences. However, our unbalanced world is such that what should go without saying often needs to be said, and the most erroneous ideas are always liable to appear the most convincing when someone omits to dot the i's and cross the t's.

We must add that the positive aspects of the constant tradition of the Church concerning the ministry (or rather ministries) of woman are often very little known or understood, and to this day can even legitimately be seen as still too inexplicit and undefined. It is therefore not only desirable but necessary to show that the negative consequences of the preceding lines of argument are neither the only ones nor the most important.

Yet it is very clear that if man, *vir*, is defined within bisexual humanity as being representative of transcendence—more explicitly, the transcendence of a God who is revealed and communicated to us in his Son made flesh of our flesh, taken on in the womb of a woman—it is not a matter of meaningless chance that he became a man and not a woman, and that, further, he called into association with himself in his mission apostles of the same sex—a mission which has been continued up to our time by bishops and priests who have also been men. At the risk of raising tempests of virtuous indignation, let us say bluntly that it would have been monstrous if the Son of God had become a woman, and that it would consequently be a total contradiction to wish that he be represented among us by both men and women without distinction, in his work of revealing the Father and of reconciliation.

On the other hand, it was only by a woman that he was able to be born among us, as one of us. And if, as St. Thomas made clear, following the whole of patristic tradition since St. Irenaeus, it was the role of the Virgin Mary not only to give him our flesh, but, by her *fiat*, to involve the freedom of all humanity in a salvation which otherwise would not truly have saved us,[36] neither is it here a matter of mean-

[36] *Summa Theologica*, Pars tertia, quaest. 30, art. 1.

ingless chance that this role fell upon a woman and not a man.

In the same way, let us add, it was not without reason that the Evangelists insisted on the role held by women, whether in the immediate preparation for the coming of the Messiah—by Elizabeth's faith, anticipating visions by a sort of tactile apprehension,[37] and in the invincible hope of the prophetess Anna[38]—or by the receptive welcome his words were given by the humble and penitent love of Mary Magdalene,[39] by the sinner at the house of Simon,[40] or by Mary of Bethany.[41]

If it falls to man rather than to woman to represent the gift of God in the transcendence of the giver, it belongs to woman no less, we repeat, not only to represent but to realize the immanence of the gift: its reception in the deepest levels of our being, from the flesh to the spirit. It was by the divine Spirit that the Word was made flesh, as it is by the same Spirit that he consummated the redemptive oblation of himself to the invisible Father while still in the flesh.[42] It is not, therefore, in vain that, after having overshadowed by his consecrating pres-

[37] Luke 1:41 and 44.
[38] Luke 2:36 ff.
[39] Matthew 28:1 and parallels, and also John 20:18.
[40] Luke 7:40 ff.
[41] Luke 10:39 and John 11.
[42] Cf. Luke 1:35 and Hebrews 9:14.

ence the Virgin who was to give birth while remaining a virgin, this Spirit allowed the same Virgin Mother and the other holy women to remain silently in the shadow of the cross at the moment when the most peremptory of the apostles defected, the most outspoken denied him, and only one single disciple, unnamed and called the beloved, remained with them after the Son of God had commended to him as his own mother her whom the Spirit had made the Mother of God.[43]

What great meaning, finally, is assumed by the fact that, even though the apostles were the only ones who officially and publicly witnessed to the resurrection, it was again the women who were the first to believe in it. So that the very message which the apostles would soon be preaching to the entire world was one which at first impressed them as the babbling of foolish women.[44]

They did not, however, begin their task of announcing and dispensing the divine mysteries without having received the Spirit, and it was grouped around Mary and these same women that they awaited and received his power. Similarly, it was in the presence of her who from the beginning had kept and pondered all these things in her heart that the last and greatest in-

---

[43] Matthew 27:55 and parallels and John 19:25 ff.
[44] Matthew 28 and parallels. Cf. John 20.

terpreter of the Gospel message set down what we might call the "definitive version."[45]

It is quite typical that the Church of the Fathers, which confirmed the practice of reserving the apostolic function to men as well as the succession of this function in the bishops and presbyters, nonetheless maintained that the vocation and the sanctity of Mary surpassed not only the priests, but even that of the angels highest in glory and those most prestigious in their ministry among the elect.[46]

However, we must emphasize that the primitive Church was persuaded that what she recognized in Mary as unique and unsurpassable was something with which all believing women were called to associate themselves through diverse vocations, in complementary ministries. Thus, alongside the apostolic ministry, there is perpetuated among us until the end of time this other ministry, inaugurated on earth by the Virgin Mary at the marriage of Cana and continued by her in heaven until the marriage of the Lamb, as all of Catholic tradition affirms.

The ministry of the apostles and their successors is a ministry of representation: sent by the Word, they are bearers, in their preaching, of its

---

[45] Luke 9:19 and 51; Acts of the Apostles 1:14; John 19:26 ff.

[46] Already present in St. John Damascene, the theme becomes classic in post-iconoclastic theology, in particular in St. Theodore the Studite.

permanent relevance. In the sacramental celebration they extend to our time its immediate reality even to us, and, by this fact, though they are simply lambs in the herd of the eternal Shepherd, they exercise in his name the pastoral function which remains wholly his. The ministry, or rather ministries, of woman are, like that of the Virgin, essentially ministries of intercession, in the broadest and deepest sense. That is to say, they have the task of drawing us to the reception of the gift of God by loving contemplation of the mystery which is dispensed to them as to us by the apostles and their successors, and beyond that of leading us into the assimilation of this mystery by living faith exercised in charity.

It is these last two ministries that the ancient Church recognized in what she very early on considered the order of consecrated virgins on the one hand, and that of deaconesses and widows on the other. It is appropriate here to examine more closely, in the light of the preceding considerations, all the meaning contained in these two fundamentally feminine "orders."

The virgins, doubtless, were not the object of a fully developed liturgical and quasi-sacramental consecration until after the development of both masculine and feminine monasticism.[47] But it is very characteristic that

---

[47] On the consecration of virgins and the theology

the liturgy of their consecration still reflects what was clear in the preceding centuries: that the virgin consecrating herself to the Lord by her commitment to perpetual virginity is much more than, and completely different from, a feminine expression of a type of ascetic life pursued indifferently by Christian men or women. In her, the Church is represented and anticipated par excellence in her eschatological realization. Limited as she may be by the bounds of a particular personality, one might still say that this anticipation already encompasses all future reality. Consecrated to Christ, the virgin becomes in effect the spouse of the Second Adam, the ultimate man. In him, humanity is able to realize itself totally by adhering, belonging, identifying itself with the transcendent model of man, the eternal Son. In the virgin bride of Christ, then, this all-encompassing virtuality, containing *in potentia*, as belongs to feminine nature in its integrity, all the possibilities proper to what is human and creaturely, far from being mutilated by the deliverance of her whole being to such a Spouse, becomes thereby perfectly actualized.

Obviously, all the multicolored variety of divine Wisdom's external plan for creation cannot be realized in an individual as it will be in the whole Church. Yet this variety finds itself,

---

which it implies, see René Metz, *La Consécration des vierges dans l'Eglise romaine* (1954).

as it were, maternally enveloped, nourished, prefigured by the purity and integrity of created love responding to the uncreated in a womanly heart. For the heart of woman, of every woman, is potentially as vast as the world, since its nature is to envelop all human and created reality. A spontaneous, essentially limitless cosmic sympathy is, as we have said, a property of feminine consciousness. If therefore this consciousness, in a total abandonment of the heart, comes to espouse the very consciousness of the Son of God made man, there awakens there something like an anticipatory echo of all that will ever be known by created consciousness raised to the level of the uncreated—in the fusion of all hearts in the universal heart of the God-Man.

This is why it has always been considered as the proper, irreplaceable, fundamental function of the virgins consecrated to Christ to be for the whole mystical body a living testimony of praise to his glory: in other words, to live perpetually in loving contemplation and adoration of the mystery of Jesus as the mystery of God revealing and communicating himself to man. "Mary pondered all these things in her heart," and, in the same way, it is the task, the specific work, of the consecrated virgin to be in her purity and totality—in her totality by the consecration of her purity—the living consciousness of the Church, as it were. Living from now on only for Christ, it falls to her in a privileged way to live in the intimate sphere of the eternal exchanges between the Father and the Son—within the movement of the Spirit of life which proceeds from the Father, rests on the Son, and recapitulates in the Son and, with him, all things, *ad Patrem*.

To the bishops and priests belongs the essentially masculine function of being the apostles of him who is himself the primordial apostle, the One sent by the Father, in whom he makes himself present to us, by the Word preached with authority, by the sacraments celebrated in the name of him who sends them, by the pastoral responsibility of which they become the instruments. But this function would be deprived of its effectiveness and, in fact, of any content which could be assimilated, without the silent cooperation of the consecrated virgin, with her fundamentally feminine function. It is she who constitutes the witness of the Spirit par excellence—that is to say, of the whole reality of the growth of divine charity in human hearts which attests to the reality of the communication of this Spirit.

Certainly, the Spirit is present and at work among the entire ecclesiastical hierarchy of ministers, and at the same time is diffused among all the members of Christ, men or women. But this ministry of the consecrated virgin—certainly not exclusively, but in an exemplary way—attests to this presence in anticipating all its eschatological fruit. Once again, her experiences can and must be shared by other Christians, whatever their sex. But it is to women in general, and in particular to the virgin exclusively and totally vowed to Christ, that it belongs first of all and most properly. All others (including men, beginning with the most elevated in the apostolic hierarchy) are drawn into this preserve by a maternal communication, in the most profound sense of maternity.

Let us repeat that it is not by chance that it was women and not men, not even the apostles, who remained at the foot of the cross, and women again who were the first to believe, and whose faith inspired or gave birth to the faith of the apostles themselves—from John, the disciple Jesus loved, to Peter, the head of the apostles. In the same way, the apostolic ministry, called to be continued until the end of time by the succession of bishops and the cooperation of priests, would be without effect, would have little or no echo, would ultimately transmit nothing, without the profound assimilation of its content: the all-powerful intercession of living faith, the faith which approaches, though in obscurity, its realization, the faith which appeared in the Virgin Mary and continues resplendent in all the consecrated virgins who have come after her—certainly too in all the faithful, but led, accompanied and enveloped by these women.

The properly paternal sacrament of the episcopal and presbyteral order represents the fatherly function in the Church which, incarnate through and in its head, Christ, encompasses the whole priestly order. This order has as its counterpart the consecration of virgins (i.e., the consecration of the womanly freedom of creation, espousing the masculine liberty of the Creator), which is the sacramental par excellence. For it is the expression which realizes this *ex opere operantis Ecclesiae*, for lack of which the divine power of the *ex opere operato* of the sacraments, whatever their efficacy, would find no welcome in the heart of man. The all-powerful motherly intercession, which is above all that of the Virgin, the Mother of God, communicates and extends itself throughout the entire Church. With a supplication inspired by and breathed in the eucharistic prayer, such intercession envelops all the still-unformed intentions of us who are believers and in whom Christ only begins to be formed.

Along with the original womanly ministry of the consecrated virgin, the early Church, beginning in apostolic times, also recognized that of "widow"—more or less synonymous with that of the deaconess.[48] The problem posed by

---

[48] There is no good modern study on this twofold subject. But one can find all the texts in the publications of Wilhelm Loehe, the founder of the Lutheran deaconesses, where he justified his resurrecting this order in Protestantism.

this lack of distinction needs to be raised, as well as that posed by the lack of distinction between the male and female diaconate. Their common solution can only be found in a clear elucidation of womanly ministries in general, which cannot be attempted without a deepened understanding of the mystery of woman.

We must observe first of all that the attempts, already made in the early Church, to find a real distinction between the male and female diaconate were unfruitful, and are destined to remain so. They are based, in effect, on the idea, having no basis in apostolic tradition, that the diaconate is an inchoative though incomplete participation in the priestly ministry: a sort of embryonic priesthood, arrested before the completion of its development. This idea arose from a faulty interpretation of the practice which seems to have become prevalent very early: that of not conferring the status of bishop or priest upon any of the faithful except those previously tested by the exercise of the diaconate. It is clear, nevertheless, that the deacon, like the lesser ministers who simply shared his secondary tasks—as opposed to the priest or bishop—did not receive by his ordination any power to accomplish anything any baptised and confirmed Christian could not do—indeed, must do in certain circumstances and, in fact, did do in the absence of a deacon or where there was an insufficient number of deacons.

Traditional Feminine Ministries

The deacon ordinarily assists the bishop or priest at the celebration of the Eucharist by leading the prayer of the faithful as well as bearing their gifts to the altar or helping the priest to redistribute them after they have been consecrated. Extraordinarily, by mandate of the bishop, he may preach or celebrate baptism. But there is no doubt that what he does ordinarily any layman could do extraordinarily and even, in a case of urgent necessity, that which even the deacon does extraordinarily. Any layman can, in fact, in certain cases, preach or give baptism, and all the more exercise the functions which derive from preaching, such as catechetical instruction or spiritual direction of others among the faithful.

The deacon is, therefore, simply consecrated to the regular exercise of those functions in the Church by which the common ministry, let us say even the common priesthood of the faithful, is connected to the ministerial priesthood and is nourished by it as by food. Every one of the faithful is, in fact, called to pray the prayer of faith which is the heart's openness to the divine Word, and which culminates in the eucharistic prayer. Likewise, all the faithful are called to offer the very thing which will be the matter of the eucharistic sacrifice, by which the design of this word is to be realized in us: the nourishment of our natural life. Finally, we are called to participate in this food transsubstantiated into the Bread of Eternal Life: the very flesh and blood of Christ, by which we all become the Body of Christ and thus are able to "make up what is lacking in the sufferings of Christ for his body, the Church, in our own bodies."

Only the bishop, however, with the priests as his helpers can preach the Word with the authority, the actual reality of Christ himself —the Word of God made flesh—and, therefore, only they can preside in his name at the eucharistic prayer, where his body is consecrated by that same Word whereby he delivers himself to us and for us in such a way that we are all encompassed in his offering as we are all gathered into him.

These two ministries—the universal ministry of all the members of the body and the particular ministry of those who are the representatives of the perpetual presence of the Head without which the body would not be able to subsist—are so closely linked to each other that neither would be able to be exercised, or even to exist, without the other: neither the Church without the bishop nor the bishop without the Church. To conjoin them is, therefore, not properly speaking a supplementary function: it is simply of the nature of the body to lend itself to that, and those who apply themselves to it more particularly do nothing more than exercise in and for the body what belongs to it as a whole, since it is a body in which all its members spontaneously cooperate even if all cannot ordinarily exercise such a function, although each individual may do so if there is a need.

Considering this, it does not seem that any essential distinction can be made between the male and female diaconate, even if the ways in which they are exercised might differ more or less according to circumstances. As neither, in fact, ever does anything more than every believer, man or woman, may do when necessary, it is difficult to see any basis for this distinction.

In fact, even if only vestiges of the female diaconate exist any more (in the West, despite recent efforts which have not yet borne much fruit, the situation of the male diaconate has for a long time not been much better), there appears even among these no trace of such a distinction. The Carthusian nuns are alone in the Latin Church in still having ordained deaconesses, who have always worn the maniple and stole, publicly sung the Gospel, and have been allowed, at least in principle, to distribute communion. The same can be said of the abbesses of the Maronite rite, and more generally of other women religious among whom similar privileges have been preserved.

In the early Church, however, it appears that the principal liturgical functions of deaconesses were the exercise among women, particularly in relation to baptismal initiation, of the same functions·as the deacons exercised among men.

Moreover, inspired explicitly by what the Acts of the Apostles tells us of the seven associated with Stephen, the early Church always considered it a function of deacons, no less essential than their liturgical functions and closely linked to their presenting the offertory gifts and distributing communion, to exercise public charity in the Church and in her name, particularly by coming to the aid of the poor. By taking care of all the material aid the Church could offer to her members in need, indeed also to non-Christians, the deacon is the first witness of the extension of that charity, supernatural but completely incarnate, which is at the heart of the Gospel message.

Here we encounter the confusing and more or less complete identification in the early Church of the female diaconate with the ministry of widows. It can be easily understood if we recall the apostolic exhortation not to admit into the ecclesiastical order of widows, recognized as such by the Church, any except those who in marriage have raised their children properly and have practiced hospitality particularly with regard to the saints (I Timothy 5:9 ff.).

What does this mean? First of all, for the women who were not called to virginal consecration, that their life in Christian marriage was to have been, in the home, like an apprenticeship to this ministry of public charity, to which the widow, consecrated as such, was then called, in participation with the ministry of the Church with regard both to its own members and those outside and in conformity with the truly Christian spirit of charity. Secondly, it means that there is, in the exercise of this charity and certainly also in its material realization, a maternal aspect which those who have experienced natural motherhood in a fully Christianized sense would be particularly apt to manifest.

Thus one might say that as the male diaconate has, since the beginning of the Church, in a way seminally contained and synthesized from the outset all the particular ministries both inside and outside the Church that lay Christian men could be called to fill, centering on and extending from those directly rooted in the Eucharist, the same has been the case for the feminine diaconate among Christian lay women.

It is very revealing, however, that there has never been felt a need to subdivide the female diaconate into specialized ministries, as was the case everywhere, both in the East and the West, with the male diaconate. For it is proper to man, *vir*, to realize himself by adopting a public role, a specialized profession which transcends his personality, whether a role within organized human society, in the state or the Church, or the representation of a properly divine role, as is the case with the priesthood or the episcopate. On the other hand, it is proper to the feminine personality, insofar as it is feminine, to define itself not by some particularity which tends to abstract from the cosmic and human community, but rather by a faculty suited to in some way bearing this community in its entirety within herself, enveloping it in the most intimate and quasi-physical sense with a solicitude not at all exterior, but rather comprehensive.

It is clear that this does not exclude for woman, on the plane of either grace or nature, the possibility of a specialized vocation—at least certain ones. But, underlying these, her maternal vocation always remains, which she brings to realization either literally in a home or analogically in a domain larger than that of the family. And, we must add, in the very exercise of vocations which woman can exercise as well as man, beginning with the diaconate, but extending to teaching, medicine, indeed even to the exercise of judiciary, political or simply administrative functions, her tasks will be to introduce into them that character of maternal empathy with those in whose interests she is working. Only woman can bring this dimension to bear in all the human activities in which she engages, in just the same sense that it is up to her alone to realize efficaciously and completely the spousal character of response to creative activity which is the supreme, ultimate vocation of every creature and of all creation.

CONCLUSION

The objection might be made to the preceding observations that they are based upon symbolic considerations. But to make such an objection would be to forget that all of Biblical revelation, and beyond that the whole sacramental economy, which tends toward the realization of the divine plan for creation, revealed to us in the Word of God, rests on what is fundamentally symbolic in that creation itself, and particularly in human nature. Contemporary psychologists tell us rightly that the crisis with which humanity is struggling today both as a whole and in each man in particular can be attributed above all to the rejection or the misunderstanding of the inborn symbolism of our being and that of the world. For the Church to adapt to this deficiency under the pretext of adapting to the modern world would only prevent her from bringing the world the very thing it most needs today. At the same time, she would be obstructed in the channels of her own proper life of grace, effectively incarnated in a humanity which God created in such a way that it is adapted to this from the outset.

It must be said once again that we are the first to recognize all the insufficiencies and indeed the possible inexactitudes of the present rough sketch. It is our opinion, however, that we do not exaggerate the importance of our work in asking those who read it not to make these weaknesses a pretext for brushing aside the questions posed here, for these questions are questions which are latent in all the reality of human existence and of which Christian revelation has simply revealed the great urgency.

For revelation was formulated for us only in such a way that at the same time unsuspected depths in nature were revealed.

We are all the more conscious that in limiting ourselves to displaying what appear to us as the essentials from the tradition on this matter, we have not even begun to draw from it the multiple applications, whether entirely new or simply renewed, which the present situation in the Church and the world demands. What the Church has done in the past is certainly far from exhausting her present and future possibilities. But to reflect as we have tried to do on the Word of God and all the experience of the Church since the apostles, while shedding light on that which must condemn deviating ways as dead ends in advance, suffices already, we believe, to demonstrate the riches which await us in apparently hidden ways, which are nevertheless the only ways of the Gospel, the only ways which correspond to the instinctive thrust of created nature such as God willed it in order to make it his own.

Abbaye de la Lucerne
31 July 1976

APPENDIX

We have preferred to limit ourselves in the body of this work to sketching the broad outlines of the most ancient and constant tradition of the Church concerning woman and her ministries. These fundamental ideas must be considered, we believe, by anyone who wants today to reflect on this problem in a serious way. But because they are so neglected, or simply ignored, we wanted to avoid the risk of weakening them, of reducing their import by mixing them, however little, with considerations or suggestions which are personal to us. However, it might be good here to give at least some glimpse of possibilities as yet unexploited, especially those proper to our time, suggested by perspectives opened by the foregoing study. A renewed appreciation, first of all, of the value of consecrated virginity, the traditional meaning of which we have recalled, already lends itself to much more creativity than is apparent at first glance. Then, too, a renovation of the female diaconate, just like that of the male diaconate, and perhaps even more so, should today be much more than a simple restoration: it should be a creative development with manifold implications. But above all, it seems to us, we must begin with a better understanding of what women accomplished in the Church in the past and of what this implies with respect to possibilities offered to or by women in the Church. We must then open our eyes to the wide range of possibilities, still largely unexplored and even less put into practice, which appear to be theirs in our society.

It is in order to present a brief sketch of these possibilities that we have included this appendix, with the understanding that here, as opposed to what has preceded, we are not claiming to set forth the authentic teaching of Biblical revelation and ecclesiastical tradition, but simply to propose some views, inspired by those same sources, which seem to us relevant to the present situation. However, we clearly realize that they may well disconcert not only those Christians who today call themselves traditionalists but also those who believe themselves to be progressives, even when the former simply maintain rigidly very recent and often aberrant customs and the latter merely return to pre-Christian and indeed pre-Biblical errors.

And we also freely recognize how much in these views is necessarily provisory, and therefore uncertain, indeed perhaps erroneous. That is why we have restricted them to the appendix: not that the problem of drawing the *nova* from the *vetera* in a spirit of living tradition is secondary, but because we are aware of the difficulties of the task and we are far from believing that what follows is gospel, nor do we wish in any sense to present it as such.

1. *Legislation and Influence*

Before going into the questions we have just enumerated, we must turn our attention to a sociological finding too little known among modern man, particularly in our civilization, which is so often irrational but no less rationalistic for all that. It is that the reality of social life always goes beyond institutional forms, and often makes light of them. It is perfectly true that the society in which we still live, particularly in France, although everything in it is unsettled or crumbling, remains substantially, on the level of expressly formulated laws, a last or next-to-last avatar of the society which the Napoleonic Code claimed to have created *ab ovo*. And it is certain that, at least on paper, society was pervaded with masculinity which was suffocating for women.[1]

---

[1] To say, as it is often said, that this thereby belies the society's archaic character, is not to know what one is talking about. It is sure, however, that in what concerns women as in what concerns the working class and peasants, it represents a resurgence of the type of societies present in Greek antiquity. But this post-Napoleonic society is nonetheless far behind, for example, the Latin society, which, in fact, recognized and (what is worth more

So much the better that people, therefore, react vigorously against that! (As long as they do not believe, once again, that women will gain the emancipation they dream of simply by being constrained to become female versions of men.) And so, just as it is impossible to believe that legislation which appears to be the most paralyzing would suffice to annihilate the actual contribution of women to society, so also we should not be under any illusions about the extent and importance of the new possibilities which are offered to them even by the most desirable changes in this domain. Proclaiming the equality of all men and women will no more make this equality a reality than denying it would suppress it.

We would even say that to imagine the contrary is a particularly masculine type of illusion. The male adores juridical labels, but he often proves incapable of filling his legal fictions with real content. Women often do without them quite well, for they naturally prefer the reality of power to its appearances. That is why the very societies where women are nothing but perpetual minors, if not slaves, must be more closely scrutinized. It suffices, in this regard, to recall the history of the Ottoman Empire to discover with what ease the exclusive reign of the male, indeed a theoretical "superman,"

---

than all the "declarations of rights" with no solid economic basis) assured in practice an astonishing independence to women.

could in fact conclude with a dictatorship of the harem!

To return to the West and to the heart of the problems of the Church, I cannot forget a conversation I had a short time ago with a Reverend Mother Abbess, who was particularly bitter against the constraints and restraints of the Code of Canon Law. "But after all, Father!" she exclaimed, "Does the Church believe us women so incapable of exercising authority that she surrounds what she allows us of it with so many reservations?"

"Do you not believe, Reverend Mother," I answered her, "that she knows you to be so gifted in the exercise of this authority that she found it prudent to provide some reins in giving it to you?"

My questioner had enough good sense to break into laughter, knowing too well, and from experience, that everywhere a female monastery exists in association with a male one, under the supposed superiority of the cowl over the wimple, it is "Reverend Mother" in reality who, not content with regulating everything in her own domain, ordinarily presides over almost everything in her neighbors' as well.

To return to more general observations, more pertinent to the laity: are not these males, filled with the awareness of their privileges, and foregoing no occasion to recall them, three-fourths of the time abject slaves of those women who appear ecstatically to accept their subordinate condition? Molière, and even more Voltaire, had a few things to say about this state of things which should long since have opened the eyes of the male sex, if their happy complacency was not above all else the result of their blindness. I refer you without pressing the matter further to the last lines of *L'Homme aux quarante écus*.

I know perfectly well the furor that such observations habitually unleash among the current brand of feminists. But I persist nonetheless (with male obstinacy!) in the unshakeable certitude that the only probable result of this kind of emancipation of woman would amount to her trading the reality for its shadow.

This does not at all mean that one must not correct, in the legislation of the Church as in that of the State, or simply in matters of custom, everything that does constitute oppression or diminution of the possibilities of truly feminine action. But it is even more important not to misunderstand the importance of real influence, no less great than that of legislation, throughout human life in general, and in the life of women in particular. So it is vital to grasp the fact that masculine efficacy is rather in the domain of formal prescription, while feminine efficacy is above all in that of influence. Without at all minimizing the importance of institutional modifications, such as those we are going to suggest, we must not fall into that form of feminism which is nothing but that of women unconsciously riveted to males to the point that they can no longer conceive of any other means of affirming their place under the sun than those which men have forged: apparent successes which, all things considered, may well be quite illusory.

2. *The Consecrated Virgin in Today's World*

An historical truth brought to light very effectively by René Metz in his work on the *Consecratio virginum* is that the consecrated virgin, as such, had a recognized place in the Church long before the appearance of the monastic movement. When this latter was developed, on the other hand, it is true that it favored the institutionalization of this consecration. But we might ask ourselves if it did not also reduce the image of the consecrated virgin, first to that of a monastic, respectable as it might be, then to that of the "religious," and finally of the "good sister," whom it is superfluous to characterize and who escapes all definition.

To this situation, or rather this progressive decline of the value placed upon the idea of consecrated virginity, clearly no remedy can be offered by an aggiornamento which has sometimes consisted for sisters in disguising themselves as glamour girls in order to explore more easily, with similarly secularized "priests", what our modern laxists amusingly call the "third way". What is necessary on the other hand, above all, is a rediscovery and a recasting of the status of the Christian virgin in the Church. It is only after this that the feminine monastic vocation can be regenerated and, more generally, a radical reform of what we call "religious" can be envisaged, which will preserve them perhaps—at least for a certain time—from turning into some new variety of "demi-saints".

But even more than this rediscovery and before this reform, a fundamental ministry of woman in the Church must emerge, no less important in its way than the priestly ministry, and its indispensable complement. I would immediately add that it would be most advantageous to maintain a jealous independence with regard to the latter, certainly along the lines of that which is most attractive in contemporary femininity: woman's desire no longer to cling to man, which is the reverse side of her ability to do without him.

In view of the erotomania of contemporary civilization, which is that of perpetual adolescence when it is not a regression to an infantile sado-anal state, I do not think the Church can do anything more healthy and health-restoring than finally to develop in all its possible dimensions woman's first and most elevated ministry.

In fact, our permissive society is breaking down from below as it lies full length in the enormous pool of its cheap pleasures. Kierkegaard had already said that, "while our ancestors were ready to throw themselves on their knees to gain their salvation, we would like to have it, like water and gas, on every floor at the mere turn of a faucet..." Woman, even more than man, is the victim of this, for she finally becomes the simple object of this pleasure for whose attainment there is no longer any desire to make even the least effort.

In contrast to what has always been the case, it is no longer prostitution which offers a substitute for love, but marriage, which tends to be reduced to a form of domestic concubinage. In fact, all these frenetic activities generously baptized "erotic," are nothing more than sad collective sessions of masturbation.

In the face of such a deterioration, the best thing the Church can do for the world would be to show it that there is no true and lasting happiness without asceticism, and no fruitful asceticism without an interior life. But what can we expect from the Church if increasing numbers no longer pray and no longer fast? It is certainly not such a Church that can drive out these demons.

On the contrary, it is essential to the Christian virgin to be the witness par excellence of that which can restore human integrity at the same time as openness to God: the voluntary renunciation motivated by faith. It should then be clear that, at a time when so many priests are no longer capable of being the first among the faithful of the religion they still pretend to represent, the only serious hope for bringing humanity back to health and restoring to it a witness of Christian sanctity which will touch it right at the seat of its evil lies in a reactivation of this virginal witness.

But be clear about this. It is not a matter of some exhibitionism of virtue succeeding to the former one of shamelessness. Witness has nothing to do with showmanship. To use one of the slogans of theological word-games of a while back, it is a question of "presence" (which is, as we have seen, entirely feminine) and not of "apostolate" (which is a vocation for men—at least insofar as emasculating rationalizations do not confuse apostolate with apostasy).

In this our world, the beings most fragile, menaced and nevertheless most capable of new independence are single women, whose number has been multiplied by the dissolution of the family. The witness of the Christian virgin which, after or along with martyrdom, was already in antiquity the motive of conversions to Christ, must surely be revived under rejuvenated forms.

I am perfectly aware of the snickering this proposition will provoke, beginning with the camp of professional feminists. "The salvation of Church and world by the old maids!" we will be told by these so-called emancipated women.

Let me then make it clear from the start that the first condition to be put upon the exercise of this regenerated ministry of the Christian virgin is that it attract girls who would not have had any more difficulty, and perhaps less, than many others in finding husbands, and that their consecration, while making them "take down their sign," as St. Francis de Sales picturesquely put it, will not transform them thereby into so many pitiful pearls. But I do not hesitate to add that there are vocations which are manifested through the pressure of ineluctable circumstances as well as by completely spontaneous inspiration. In other words, many unmarried women who only remained so because they had no choice in the matter, if they have the courage, may very well come to the point, not only of ratifying, but of transfiguring a sad necessity into such a joyous conviction that it finally becomes no less convincing than that of their sisters favored with the gifts of nature, if not of grace.

Poverty having been always the necessary accompaniment of consecrated virginity, or, rather, consecrated virginity being itself no more than the consummated interiorization of Scriptural poverty, how are we to conceive the forms it should take today for the virgin united to Christ? We do not have far to look: typist, seamstress, salesgirl in a department store, nurse or laboratory worker, etc. These and other professions offer more than enough choices for them to earn their bread by the sweat of their brows, without great risk of falling into the excesses of our consumer society. Since the usual possibility of living "protected" in the womb of the family, which was the recourse of virgins of antiquity, is no longer much more than a dream or a memory, it would be permissible to our modern virgins either to live together in twos and threes in a modest apartment or to opt for solitude, which certainly demands more courage, but can, after all, prove to be even less trying.

Without necessarily entering into all the already over-complicated machinery of the contemporary secular institutes, these could also share with freer associations the simplest and best of their experience. On these bases it is desirable, while seeking all the good advice available, but without committing themselves to follow it always (since it is a question of women, there is little danger of this happening), that they make their rules of life for themselves rather than receiving them ready-made from some "good priest."

Certainly, it would be good for them to profit freely from all that ecclesiastics who are capable of understanding them can provide, particularly on the level of doctrine and confessions. But what spiritual direction they need could often be more advantageously given them by their companions or more experienced sisters than by the best-intentioned clerics or religious.

Considering some of the aberrations of the contemporary clergy and its return at breakneck speed to the mores and customs of the fifteenth century, under the guise of progressivism, it would be much to their advantage not to mix too much in these circles if they value their consecration—and, as a matter of fact, their virtue.

In ideal circumstances which, obviously, our present circumstances can hardly be construed to be, their parish church should be their chapel. Barring that, they will certainly discover with a little luck and, if possible, a small car, some place, monastic or not, where people still pray in the Catholic fashion and where the "Eucharist" is celebrated in a manner which makes it possible to recognize it as a Catholic Mass.

But, one might ask, what would be, with all this, the "ministry" of these virgins? Essentially to pray—to pray at church and at home, in such a way that they move toward praying without ceasing, carrying in prayer their whole existence and that of all those around them, a prayer in which their total donation to God in Christ, head and members, is ceaselessly expressed and renewed, which only total renunciation of all that is not Him renders truly effective.

It is this witness, and, beyond the witness, this mysterious bringing Christ to birth in others by association with his Cross in the eucharistic spirit, which will always constitute, as it has always constituted, the proper ministry of the consecrated virgin. Let us not hesitate to say it again: it is just as essential to the Church and the world as the priestly ministry. And it has perhaps never been more obviously necessary.

Let no one answer that all this is utopian. To be sure, it has no place in the sacrosanct and empty cadres of specialized Catholic Action—nor in those of the "great orders" or of the more modest congregations. But it already exists and is much more widespread than one might think. I would even be tempted to say that this form of consecrated life already has its saint, who can easily do without canonization: Madeleine Delbrêl. If one reads *Nous autres gens des rues* one will see that I have not simply made this up. This will permit me to pass from the consecrated virgin as such to the monastic and the religious, as one would wish them to become again—or become for the first time!

3. *Religious Vocations Today*

The monastics constitute traditionally the milieu par excellence from which liturgically consecrated virgins are drawn. More exactly, if she has come to the monastery in what the canon lawyers call *integritas corporis*, the nun is called to receive this consecration as the crowning of her religious life definitively constituted on the base of the solemn profession. It is not amiss to compare this with the professed monk who then can and, in fact, often does receive the priesthood.

The nun, in fact, like the monk for his part among the baptized of the masculine sex, is no more than a baptized woman who undertakes to realize, as immediately and totally as possible, all that baptism renders desirable. She does this by the means that baptism itself indicates and which are not in general more than an application of the cross of Christ to all of life, with a view to an anticipated communion with his resurrection.

In this regard, there is nothing clerical about either the monk or the nun. In principle, they are no more than laymen particularly "involved," as people like to say today, but not in some political cause, simply rather, in the Christianity of the Gospel.

After that, work, according to the best monastic tradition, is the first of all the ascetic practices and the basis of all the others. And there is hardly a human task that can be assumed by a woman that the nun cannot make hers, so long as it can be accomodated to her vocation to a thoroughly evangelical life.

Understood thus, the monastic life of

women, as well as of men, far from being a life apart and although it must be energetically separated from life as the world knows and practices it, is a life whose concrete realization in a group which is communally consecrated to it should normally furnish a center where the laity (continuing to live in the world and beginning with the consecrated virgins who are not monastics) come to revive their zeal by deepening their faith and their prayer. (Even some priests might do this, but, in our day, one must not expect too much!)

In this primordial task of hospitality—a total hospitality offered to the soul as well as the body, fatigued by our existence—which is often hectic and too often devoid of meaning—there is no doubt that nuns faithful to the spirit as well as to the letter of their "holy rules," as they say, would be much more easily and widely efficacious than men, even those of indisputable sanctity. If you ask why, the answer is quite simple: as the ants have their hills and the bees their hives, so women quietly make their "homes," as naturally as men, assembled even for the most sublime motives, tend regularly either to the mixture of militarism and laxity found in the barracks, or to the exclusive comfort of a club for old bachelors. (It is not I who say this: it is the most learned modern Benedictine commentator on the Rule of St. Benedict—Dom Cuthbert Butler.)

What is one to think of the marvelous development—has it been sufficiently described to us as such in the past?—by which monks became religious, indefinitely multiplied and diversified? Is it truly a privilege of the West, while the East has hardly known such a phenomenon? Yet this proliferation is still of small proportions compared to that of women religious.

At the end of the nineteenth century, the foundation of a new congregation of women became the sign of a clerical career reaching its glorious apotheosis.

However, since at least the end of the Middle Ages, it was clear that this multiplication of "religious" men and women had as its primary effect the loss from view of the meaning of monastic life, whose essential character we have just recalled, and which appears an indispensable element to a Christianity in progress and not in decadence. Is it not clear that today all this vegetation is more than exhausted, to the point that one could not touch it without its falling into dust or decay?

Is it not the moment, leaving aside here male religious, to ask ourselves this question: would not the rebirth and transposition of the ancient order of deaconesses and widows, either within or outside of the monastic cadre, be the only realistic way of revivifying whatever deserves to survive of the "religious" of yesterday and today? We would have at the same time the chance to redevelop within the Church, beside the fundamental ministry of woman, that of the virgin consecrated to Christ in the prayer of faith and other ministries justifiably diverse, as a function of the concrete "services" which the Church and the world, today, can expect of the most fervent Christians. To wish to enter here into the details would this time be to move into utopia or would lead us too far into analyses which are not within our province. But the best that we could do was, we believe, to pose clearly the question which has just been enunciated.

And now we arrive at a conclusion which will provoke the accusation that we are simply defending a housewife feminism, from the same critics who would have seen nothing in what has preceded but a pious salvaging of the "old maids" in waiting.

Well, so be it, as long as nothing is attributed to us but what we actually say. We make no claim that the role of housewife should be the only possible ministry for women, nor the ideal ministry. We have just developed the contrary position at length.

This does not lessen the fact that the mass of women, whether Christian or not, just like the mass of men, is destined for marriage. And today as always, if there is a place where the most ordinary of women, and many of the most extraordinary, can give their full measure, and that which they alone are capable of giving, it is quite certainly, however much one might affirm the contrary, in the family which is not only theirs, but which they will have produced (yes, with the cooperation of their husbands! but with a cooperation which remains episodic and, in the best of cases, always more or less amateur: see above). Péguy, in a beautiful passage of oratory, calls the fathers of the family the adventurers of the modern world. Yes, without a doubt, but adventurers who would have every chance of caving in from thirst or hunger in the desert of the modern world, with or after their kids, if the women were not there, like Sarah in the tent, who certainly had good excuse to laugh up her sleeve. Whatever be, then, what is pompously called "action in the world," to which one would hope women, like men and Christians in the front ranks, can and must consecrate themselves: the action in the family, on the family, through the family, remains and shall always remain that of the great majority of women, and no one else will ever replace them.

There is no doubt that they must themselves envisage, prepare and create new forms in confused and confusing circumstances. But that is surely why, after having limited ourselves to clearing the way, we shall leave them to enter upon it, without pretending to teach them how.

EPILOGUE

by Hans Urs von Balthasar

It may appear presumptuous to append an epilogue to an essay as compact and bold as the preceding. We write it in the hope of doing a service to the thoughts of the author, with whose basic argument we are wholly in agreement. By adding a few complementary remarks we hope to protect the author from the attacks which he himself expects from all sides. He will not perhaps hold against his friend this attempt at offering a protective hand, especially since he has repeatedly stressed the incompleteness of his assertions and even the fact that they are open to misinterpretation.[1]

Over against Christ—man and bridegroom —the Church is decidedly and primarily feminine. In this sense we must not hesitate to

---

[1] From a wholly different direction I already ventured such protective help in my book, *Der antirömische Affekt* (1975). In it I showed that the feminine, Marian principle is, in the Church, what encompasses all other principles, even the Petrine.

characterize as "the first and preeminent office" in the Church that ecclesial ministry performed by women who represent the Church as a whole because they have consecrated their entire existence to it in a special way. But Bouyer's whole train of thought rests on an interior analogy between the natural relation of the sexes and the supernatural relation between Christ and the Church. In the natural relation, the woman enjoys the inward role of bearing, a role which is more perduring, while the man provides an external, episodic function: he merely *represents* a primal, creative principle which he himself can never *be*. And the question may be asked whether, in the abbreviated form in which it is presented by Bouyer, this analogy is really capable of carrying the burden of proof.

Let us begin by giving our hearty assent to everything the author says about the essence of woman, and to his conclusion that the ecclesial office proper is unsuited to her. Here Bouyer is saying in an original manner what, in the German-speaking world, a Gertrud von Le Fort and an Ida Friederike Görres said before him in another, no less emphatic way. His basic affirmation is that, in the sexual realm, woman is the full explicitation of the dignity bestowed on the creature of being a second causality alongside, in and through God. Because of this, furthermore, woman enjoys the role of being the world's comprehensive answer to God. The role of the man consequently acquires a peculiarly open bi-polarity where woman's role exhibits a closure: as a representative of the Creator God, the man is more than himself, and yet, at the same time, as a mere transmitter who can as such *only* represent, he is also less than himself. Once this, in my opinion, irrefutable assertion is applied to the relation between the Bride-Church (as a conceiving, bearing, birth-giving and nurturing reality) and the ecclesial ministerial office, it seems that no objection against it would hold up. And this will stand even after the following has been said.

We could ask whether in this short essay the discussion concerning Christ's essence and position is not somewhat elliptical. Is it really impossible to ascribe to Christ with regard to the Church a role which is as ephemeral as that played by the man as a sexual being with regard to the woman? The author is, of course, aware of this, and he comes to terms with it in two ways. The Church, on the one hand, is the body formed by Christ the Head and proceeding from within him. She is the coming-into-view of the fullness of Christ, who in this "body" or "bride" fashions his own fullness for himself. On the other hand, to do this is possible for him only because, as Bouyer says, the Son in the world is the sole fully valid representative of the only fatherhood perfectly deserving the name: the paternity of the eternal Father who begets the Son in one uninterrupted act and who, together with the Son and the Spirit, creates and sustains the world in just as continuous a manner. In this connection, therefore, the relationship of Christ to the Church is incomparably higher than that which, for its part, the ecclesial ministerial office can assume towards the Church as, in a way, representing Christ within and to the Church.

At this point we can ask in what this incomparability consists between the man Christ (as the representative of the Creator God) and the male ministerial office or, in the first place the male's natural sexual function. This question places us squarely before the mystery of the Cross and of the Eucharist it makes possible. Here it is that the Good Shepherd succeeds in laying down his life for his sheep in such a way that this life is handed over to his own as their indispensable and ever-available nourishment in the form of bread and wine. Jesus' whole humanity attains to such supernatural fruitfulness through the Cross that, compared to it, the man's momentary fruitfulness in the sexual act is but a shadow of an analogy. And so it must be if the Son, in his Eucharist (which is the foremost foundation of the Church's "body:" I Corinthians 10:17), is to be a true representation of the Father's eternal fruitfulness, and if at the same time, as man (as male!), he is to be the principle of the Church, which arises as Eve from Adam.

Behind all this there lies an even deeper mystery, one we hardly dare touch, since projecting our sexual differentiation onto God can only create misunderstandings, as Bouyer himself clearly shows. Nevertheless, we can still assert that the Son's mode of divinity is an eternally receptive one, and this further allows us to understand two things. First, as a man, the Son never represents himself, but always the Father, as if his humility were familiar to him already from the divine inner life of the Trinity. And second, when the Church arises from him as Eve from Adam, the Son foreknows in himself (potentially or eminently, as it were) what the feminine-active mode of receptiveness involves.

This shows us once again that all gnostic speculation about divine sexual beings (syzygies) or a hermaphroditic primal human being does indeed point in the general direction of the Trinity, and yet in so doing it totally misses the mark of the Trinitarian mystery. Both here and even more explicitly in other books, Bouyer's manner of criticizing such speculation is exemplary: he does not simply reject its basic impulse or demythologize it as merely the way the Trinity appears to us. The radical separation of feminine *Sophia* (God's plan for the world and at most, in its realization, the world's answer to God) and masculine *Logos* (which in Jesus becomes flesh) results in the perfect bridal character of both: through Christ and in the Spirit, the created world is introduced into the bridal chamber of God the Father. And Bouyer does not overlook the fact that even God's masculine Word (*memra*) has a feminine aspect: through the Word, he is implanted into creation as *Sophia*.

For us, however, the more essential question is the following: What are the implications of everything we have said about the manner in which the Son represents the Father (by being distributed in the Eucharist) for the bearer of the ecclesial priesthood? Bouyer's assertions in this essay concerning "spiritual fatherhood" impose strict limits: God alone is our Father through Christ's work. No person, not even an officially delegated one, may arrogate to himself more than the possibility of transmitting. But if we do not interpret this "spiritual fatherhood" primarily on the analogy from below (that of the sexes), but rather on the analogy from above (the Christological), then our emphases ought to be slightly shifted. "Spiritual fatherhood, which imposes on the priest his particular vocation, is so far-reaching that it can scarcely be equated wih physical fatherhood and its particular responsibilities. Once the latter has been sacrificed as is demanded, however, then there occurs what is always the case with all authentic sacrifices: one rediscovers at a higher or deeper level (the meaning is the same) the entire, precious, human reality which had been surrendered."[2]

And concerning the exodus of the first monks into the desert, Bouyer says that it was undertaken to struggle with the evil forces vicariously, for the good of the Church. But he then sends the monks "back into the world that their spiritual fatherhood might have its effect on others, since it is this fatherhood which alone merits the monk his name, and he proves this not only by his dress but by the Holy Spirit within him."[3]

Now, against all of this the final objection could be raised that the spiritual fruitfulness both of the priest and the monk (that the latter is included, not being a priest, is significant) falls to them insofar as they have a living faith and are, therefore, children of Mother Church like all laymen. This can in no way be denied, not even for the priest. Precisely at this point is

[2] *L'Eglise de Dieu* (1970) 259; cf. 345.

[3] Ibid., 564. These quotes also make clear how we are to understand Bouyer's statements about priest and woman concretely. And he says clearly enough what he thinks of all those things people are fond of calling the "third way," but which amount to a corrosion or destruction of celibacy from within. The custom of times past of having a "spiritual bride" at priests' First Masses—today mostly forgotten or reduced to external convention—witnessed to an instance of ancient Church wisdom which led no one to think of any abuse.

where we must most emphatically lend our strongest support to Bouyer's extremely fertile idea of an inseparable conjunction of the priestly ministerial office and the intercessory ministerial office, which exhibits the traits of both the virgin and the mother. With regard to the priest's "spiritual fatherhood," however, one will never be in a position of calculating which graces flow to him from the eucharistic Head whom he represents and which from the "Body" whose intercession supports him.

This non-calculable character of grace in no way invalidates the clear opposition we showed earlier between (masculine) representation and (feminine) conception that actively bears to full term. If this short epilogue appears to be something of a rehabilitation of the male in the Church (especially of the man on whom the priestly-episcopal office has been conferred), it was only our intention to set in relief a couple of key ideas which the author has himself already sketched elsewhere. We did not seek to undermine the humility which is always required of the male and which concludes the Gospel of the Beloved Disciple, united as he was to Mary. In the passage in question, Jesus must three times ask Peter, his first pope and the one who betrayed him three times, whether he loves him, before he can hand over to him the shepherd's staff.

Epilogue

So as not to close this epilogue with our own critical remarks, we have appended some refreshing reflections by a full-voiced thinker who harmonizes perfectly with Bouyer. I speak of C. S. Lewis, the great Anglican lay theologian who, in spite of being a professor of philology, was perhaps in our century the most conversant in theological matters.[4]

[4] The following essay appears in: *God in the Dock* (1970), *Essays on Theology and Ethics*, 234-239. It first appeared in "Notes on the Way," in: *Time and Tide*, v. 29 (August 14, 1948) 830-31. We gratefully acknowledge the permission of The Trustees of the Estate of C. S. Lewis to reprint this essay here.

The epilogue is from Louis Bouyer, *Frau und Kirche*, translation and epilogue by H. U. von Balthasar: (Einsiedeln: Johannes Verlag, 1977), 87-95. We are grateful to Fr. von Balthasar and Johannes Verlag for permission to include it here.

PRIESTESSES IN THE CHURCH?

by C. S. Lewis

"I should like Balls infinitely better," said Caroline Bingley, "if they were carried on in a different manner...It would surely be much more rational if conversation instead of dancing made the order of the day." "Much more rational, I dare say," replied her brother, "but it would not be near so much like a Ball."[1] We are told that the lady was silenced: yet it could be maintained that Jane Austen has not allowed Bingley to put forward the full strength of his position. He ought to have replied with a *distinguo*. In one sense conversation is more rational for conversation may exercise the reason alone, dancing does not. But there is nothing irrational in exercising other powers than our reason. On certain occasions and for certain purposes the real irrationality is with those who will not do so. The man who would try to break a horse or write a poem or beget a child by pure syllogizing would be an irrational man; though at the same time syllogizing is in itself a more rational

[1] *Pride and Prejudice*, ch. 11.

activity than the activities demanded by these achievements. It is rational not to reason, or not to limit oneself to reason, in the wrong place; and the more rational a man is the better he knows this.

These remarks are not intended as a contribution to the criticism of *Pride and Prejudice*. They came into my head when I heard that the Church of England[2] was being advised to declare women capable of Priests' Orders. I am, indeed, informed that such a proposal is very unlikely to be seriously considered by the authorities. To take such a revolutionary step at the present moment, to cut ourselves off from the Christian past and to widen the divisions between ourselves and other Churches by establishing an order of priestesses in our midst, would be an almost wanton degree of imprudence. And the Church of England herself would be torn in shreds by the operation. My concern with the proposal is of a more theoretical kind. The question involves something even deeper than a revolution in order.

I have every respect for those who wish women to be priestesses. I think they are sincere and pious and sensible people. Indeed, in a way they are too sensible. That is where my dissent from them resembles Bingley's dissent from his sister. I am tempted to say that the

[2] Called the Episcopal Church in the United States.

proposed arrangement would make us much more rational "but not near so much like a Church."

For at first sight all the rationality (in Caroline Bingley's sense) is on the side of the innovators. We are short of priests. We have discovered in one profession after another that women can do very well all sorts of things which were once supposed to be in the power of men alone. No one among those who dislike the proposal is maintaining that women are less capable than men of piety, zeal, learning and whatever else seems necessary for the pastoral office. What, then, except prejudice begotten by tradition, forbids us to draw on the huge reserves which could pour into the priesthood if women were here, as in so many other professions, put on the same footing as men? And against this flood of common sense, the opposers (many of them women) can produce at first nothing but an inarticulate distaste, a sense of discomfort which they themselves find it hard to analyze.

That this reaction does not spring from any contempt for women is, I think, plain from history. The Middle Ages carried their reverence for one Woman to a point at which the charge could be plausibly made that the Blessed Virgin became in their eyes almost "a fourth person of the Trinity." But never, so far as I know, in all those ages was anything remotely resembling a sacerdotal office attributed to her. All salvation depends on the decision which she made in the words *Ecce ancilla*;[3] she is united in nine months' inconceivable intimacy with the eternal Word; she stands at the foot of the cross.[4] But she is absent both from the Last Supper[5] and from the descent of the Spirit at Pentecost.[6] Such is the record of Scripture. Nor can you daff it aside by saying that local and temporary conditions condemned women to silence and private life. There were female preachers. One man had four daughters who all "prophesied," i.e., preached.[7] There were prophetesses even in Old Testament times. Prophetesses, not priestesses.

At this point the common sensible reformer is apt to ask why, if women can preach, they cannot do all the rest of a priest's work. This question deepens the discomfort of my side. We begin to feel that what really divides us from our opponents is a difference between the meaning which they and we give to the word "priest." The more they speak (and speak truly)

---

[3] After being told by the angel Gabriel that she has found favor with God and that she should bear the Christ Child, the Virgin exclaims "Behold the handmaid of the Lord" (Luke 1:38). The *Magnificat* follows in verses 46-55.

[4] Matthew 27:55-6; Mark 15:40-1; Luke 23:49; John 19:25.

[5] Matthew 26:26; Mark 14:22; Luke 22:19.

[6] Acts 2:1 et seq.

[7] Acts 21:9.

Priestesses in the Church?

about the competence of women in administration, their tact and sympathy as advisers, their national talent for "visiting," the more we feel that the central thing is being forgotten. To us a priest is primarily a representative, a double representative, who represents us to God and God to us. Our very eyes teach us this in church. Sometimes the priest turns his back on us and faces the East—he speaks to God for us: sometimes he faces us and speaks to us for God. We have no objection to a woman doing the first: the whole difficulty is about the second. But why? Why should a woman not in this sense represent God? Certainly not because she is necessarily, or even probably, less holy or less charitable or stupider than a man. In that sense she may be as "God-like" as a man; and a given woman much more so than a given man. The sense in which she cannot represent God will perhaps be plainer if we look at the thing the other way round.

Suppose the reformer stops saying that a good woman may be like God and begins saying that God is like a good woman. Suppose he says that we might just as well pray to "Our Mother which art in heaven" as to "Our Father." Suppose he suggests that the Incarnation might just as well have taken a female as a male form, and the Second Person of the Trinity be as well called the Daughter as the Son. Suppose, finally, that the mystical marriage were reversed, that the Church were the Bridegroom and Christ the Bride. All this, as it seems to me, is involved in the claim that a woman can represent God as a priest does.

Now it is surely the case that if all these supposals were ever carried into effect we should be embarked on a different religion. Goddesses have, of course, been worshipped: many religions have had priestesses. But they are religions quite different in character from Christianity. Common sense, disregarding the discomfort, or even the horror, which the idea of turning all our theological language into the feminine gender arouses in most Christians, will ask "Why not? Since God is in fact not a biological being and has no sex, what can it matter whether we say *He* or *She*, *Father* or *Mother*, *Son* or *Daughter*?"

But Christians think that God himself has taught us how to speak of him. To say that it does not matter is to say either that all the masculine imagery is not inspired, is merely human in origin, or else that, though inspired, it is quite arbitrary and unessential. And this is surely intolerable: or, if tolerable, it is an argument not in favour of Christian priestesses but against Christianity. It is also surely based on a shallow view of imagery. Without drawing upon religion, we know from our poetical experience that image and apprehension cleave closer together than common sense is here prepared to admit; that a child who has been taught to pray to a Mother in Heaven would have a religious life radically different from that of a Christian child. And as image and apprehension are in an organic unity, so, for a Christian, are human body and human soul.

The innovators are really implying that sex is something superficial, irrelevant to the spiritual life. To say that men and women are equally eligible for a certain profession is to say that for the purposes of that profession their sex is irrelevant. We are, within that context, treating both as neuters. As the State grows more like a hive or an ant-hill it needs an increasing number of workers who can be treated as neuters. This may be inevitable for our secular life. But in our Christian life we must return to reality. There we are not homogeneous units, but different and complementary organs of a mystical body. Lady Nunburnholme has claimed that the equality of men and women is a Christian principle.[8] I do not remember the text in scripture nor the Fathers, nor Hooker, nor the Prayer Book which asserts it, but that is not here my point. The point is that unless "equal" means "interchangeable," equality makes nothing for the priesthood of women. And the kind of equality which implies that the equals are in-

---

[8]Lady Marjorie Nunburnholme, "A Petition to the Lambeth Conference," *Time and Tide* (10 July 1948) v. 29, 720.

terchangeable (like counters or identical machines) is, among humans, a legal fiction. It may be useful legal fiction. But in church we turn our back on fictions. One of the ends for which sex was created was to symbolize to us the hidden things of God. One of the functions of human marriage is to express the nature of the union between Christ and the Church. We have no authority to take the living and semitive figures which God has painted on the canvas of our nature and shift them about as if they were mere geometrical figures.

This is what common sense will call "mystical." Exactly. The Church claims to be the bearer of a revelation. If that claim is false then we want not to make priestesses but to abolish priests. If it is true, then we should expect to find in the Church an element which unbelievers will call irrational and which believers will call supra-rational. There ought to be something in it opaque to our reason though not contrary to it—as the facts of sex and sense on the natural level are opaque. And that is the real issue. The Church of England can remain a church only if she retains this opaque element. If we abandon that, if we retain only what can be justified by standards of prudence and convenience at the bar of enlightened common sense, then we exchange revelation for that old wraith Natural Religion.

Priestesses in the Church?

It is painful, being a man, to have to assert the privilege, or the burden, which Christianity lays upon my own sex. I am crushingly aware how inadequate most of us are, in our actual and historical individualities, to fill the place prepared for us. But it is an old saying in the army that you salute the uniform not the wearer. Only one wearing the masculine uniform can (provisionally, and till the *Parousia*)[9] represent the Lord to the Church: for we are all, corporately and individually, feminine to him. We men may often make very bad priests. That is because we are insufficiently masculine. It is no cure to call in those who are not masculine at all. A given man may make a very bad husband; you cannot mend matters by trying to reverse the roles. He may make a bad male partner in a dance. The cure for that is that men should more diligently attend dancing classes; not that the ballroom should henceforward ignore distinctions of sex and treat all dancers as neuter. That would, of course, be eminently sensible, civilized, and enlightened, but, once more, "not near so much like a Ball."

And this parallel between the Church and the Ball is not so fanciful as some would think. The Church ought to be more like a Ball than it is like a factory or a political party. Or, to speak

[9] The future return of Christ in glory to judge the living and the dead.

more strictly, they are at the circumference and the Church at the Centre and the Ball comes in between. The factory and the political party are artificial creations—"a breath can make them as a breath has made." In them we are not dealing with human beings in their concrete entirety—only with "hands" or voters. I am not of course using "artificial" in any derogatory sense. Such artifices are necessary: but because they are our artifices we are free to shuffle, scrap and experiment as we please. But the Ball exists to stylize something which is natural and which concerns human beings in their entirety—namely, courtship. We cannot shuffle or tamper so much. With the Church, we are farther in: for there we are dealing with male and female not merely as facts of nature but as the live and awful shadows of realities utterly beyond our control and largely beyond our direct knowledge. Or rather, we are not dealing with them but (as we shall soon learn if we meddle) they are dealing with us.